When
FOOTBALL *Was*
FOOTBALL
CRYSTAL PALACE

First published in 2014

A catalogue record for this book is available from the British Library

ISBN: 978-0-85733-665-1

Published by Haynes Publishing, Sparkford, Yeovil,
Somerset BA22 7JJ, UK
Tel: 01963 442030 Fax: 01963 440001
Int. tel: +44 1963 442030 Int. fax: +44 1963 440001
E-mail: sales@haynes.co.uk
Website: www.haynes.co.uk

Haynes North America Inc., 861 Lawrence Drive,
Newbury Park, California 91320, USA

Images © Mirrorpix

Creative Director: Kevin Gardner
Designed for Haynes by BrainWave

Printed and bound in the US

When
FOOTBALL *Was* FOOTBALL

CRYSTAL PALACE

A Nostalgic Look at a Century of the Club

Tom Hopkinson

Contents

Foreword

I went to watch my first game of football at the age of nine with a friend and his dad and, looking back, I still find it weird that it was a Crystal Palace match at Selhurst Park.

Little did I realize that day what a huge part the club would go on to play in my life and, when I joined Palace as an apprentice just a few years later, it was a dream come true.

It is a wonderful, wonderful football club and I loved every single day I was a player there.

In time, of course, I left – Terry Venables told me one day that I was getting a new contract and two days later that he was selling me to Arsenal; he still won't tell me the truth about what went on even now, but Palace always remained dear to me, and I love going back and being involved as a match-day host.

My brother, Peter, came with me the day I signed and handled the negotiations with then-chairman Ray Bloye, and I don't think I could have joined the club at a better time.

I know Palace reached the FA Cup final with the team of Ian Wright and Mark Bright in 1990, and they had a great side, but I would still say ours was the best team in the club's history.

I'm biased, of course, but I think so many fans would say the same.

The camaraderie and atmosphere was incredible in our side, and with so many of us coming through together and creating the so-called 'Team of the 80s', we were like one big family. They were great times.

I won my first seven England caps while playing for Crystal Palace and I was proud to represent the club as well as myself when I played for my country.

We can't forget that there have been some tough times along the way, so it's good to see them doing well in recent years and I'm so pleased for the fans. The supporters are incredible and they don't get mentioned as often as they should.

During my time as a player at Palace and through all of the club's rich history, the *Mirror* and its sister papers have been there to report on the great games and great players – and the heartbreaking moments as well. The evocative pictures – taken from the *Mirror* archive – which feature in this book, have rekindled so many wonderful memories and I hope they will do the same for you.

This is a celebration of a golden age for football and a fine portrait of a wonderful football club.

Kenny Sansom

Goodman's Glaziers
1905-1915

In 1905, Aston Villa and Newcastle United contested the FA Cup final at the Palace in front of a crowd of 101,117. Villa won the game 2-0.

The Crystal Palace had been synonymous with English football for a decade, hosting FA Cup finals and England internationals on its grounds on top of Sydenham Hill in South London, before finally it could boast a team of its own. But in 1905, a year after rejecting a proposal from the Crystal Palace Company to have a team playing at the Palace and bearing its name, the FA at last approved the formation of a club. The general manager of the Palace, Mr JH Cozens, approached Aston Villa, one of the English game's leading clubs at the time, and the Midlanders' chairman William McGregor, the founding father of the Football League, gave his considerable backing to the Palace venture. It was upon McGregor's recommendation that Edmund Goodman, a young assistant secretary at Villa, was taken on, and he organized both the club and its new team. Goodman, forced to retire as a player by a knee injury which required an amputation at the age of 19, appointed John Robson as manager and found the club's first chairman, Sydney Bourne. Robson put together his team and made Ted Birnie, a former Newcastle United player, his captain. The club, nicknamed the Glaziers, would play in the Southern League Second Division, largely against the reserve teams of the country's established sides, but also in the United League as well. The United League gave Palace the chance to play against the first teams of Southern League outfits, more often than not in midweek fixtures, and really it was the Southern League Second Division fixtures which mattered. On 2nd September 1905, Palace lost their first game in that competition 4-3 to Southampton Reserves – with Charles Roberts, Archie Needham and George Thompson scoring the Glaziers' goals – but they didn't suffer another defeat all season and capped a fine debut campaign by winning promotion to Division One as champions.

BELOW: The 1914 FA Cup final, in which Burnley beat Liverpool 1-0, is captured in a photograph which ran in the *Mirror* on 14th April and shows the Crystal Palace ground in all its glory. As the caption beneath the picture reports, it was the first Cup final at which a monarch was present, with King George V presenting the triumphant Burnley captain Tommy Boyle with the trophy.

1905 Crystal Palace Football Club is formed by the Crystal Palace Company at the glass venue on Sydenham Hill. The club, under the management of John Robson, enters Southern League Division Two and plays its first match against Southampton Reserves at the Crystal Palace on 2nd September. That 4-3 defeat to the Saints' second string would prove the only stain on an otherwise fine season. The Glaziers did not lose another game in the 1905–06 campaign and were crowned champions. **1906–07** Palace enjoyed a giant-killing in the FA Cup when they beat Newcastle United 1-0 at St James' Park to record one of their most memorable victories. The Magpies went on to win the Division One championship that season, while Palace finished 19th in the Southern League First Division. **1907–08** Edmund Goodman takes over the managerial reins and will stay in charge for the next 18 years. Welshman Bill Davies, a right-winger, writes his name into club legend when he becomes the first Palace player to represent his country. **1914** Palace have an England international in their ranks when Henry Colclough becomes the club's first player to represent the Three Lions. On his debut, on 16th March, he helps England to a 2-0 victory over Wales in Cardiff. **1915** The Crystal Palace is requisitioned by the Admiralty at the outbreak of the First World War, meaning the club is forced to move to the home of West Norwood FC at Herne Hill running track. Palace, now playing at Herne Hill, move into the London Combination and remain in that league throughout the war. Sidney Sanders scores six goals in a 10-1 victory over Herne Hill on 4th March.

"I consider that the Crystal Palace should, in time, get as big as any club in the south, or even in England, that is if our team is fairly successful from a playing point of view."

Edmund Goodman

At the start of the 20th century, football did not receive the blanket coverage which it does these days, but newspaper editors still realized its importance to the nation. The *Mirror*, launched in 1903, would preview fixtures and report their results, although often just a sentence on each game would suffice. On 2nd February 1912, a report under the headline "League Clubs' Prospects" (right) said that "Crystal Palace will have to go hard to win at Coventry". It was accurate, as well: despite goals from Ernest Myers and Ted Smith, Palace were beaten 3-2.

RIGHT: The oldest surviving picture of Crystal Palace to appear in the *Mirror* ran on Monday 30th September 1905, and showed action from the Glaziers' goalless draw with East Londoners Leyton.

BELOW: The first traceable mention of Crystal Palace FC in the pages of the *Mirror*, on Saturday 2nd September 1905. Their match against Southampton Reserves, a 4-3 defeat, was recorded along with the rest of the day's fixtures.

NEWS by PHOTOGRAPHS

SATURDAY'S LEAGUE MATCHES.

TO-DAY'S MATCHES.

ASSOCIATION.

THE LEAGUE.—Division I.

Birmingham City v. Preston North End. | Notts F. v. Wolverhmptn W.
Blackburn R. v. Aston Villa | Sheffield W. v. Manchester C.
Bolton W. v. Sheffield Utd. | Stoke v. Notts C.
Derby County v. Bury. | Sunderland v. Newcastle U.
Everton v. Middlesbrough. | Woolwich A. v. Liverpool.

Division II.

Blackpool v. Burton United. | Leicester F. v. Clapton Orient
Bradford City v. Leeds City. | Lincoln C. v. Barslem P. V.
Chesterfield T. v. Grimsby T. | Manchester U. v. Bristol C.
Glossop v. Gainsbro' Trinity. | Stockport County v. Chelsea.
Hull City v. Barnsley. | W. Brom. Albion v. Burnley.

SOUTHERN LEAGUE.

Plymouth A. v. Norwich C. | West Ham U. v. Swindon.
Southampton v. Brentford. | Fulham v. Portsmouth.
Reading v. Tottenham Hot. | Queen's Park R. v. New
Brighton and H. Albion v. | Brompton.
Millwall. | Bristol Rov. v. Northampton.

Division II.

Crystal Palace v. Southampton Res. | Portsmouth R. v. Fulham R.
| Swindon R. v. W. Ham R.

SOUTH-EASTERN LEAGUE.

Grays U. v. Brighton and Hove Utd. | Leyton v. Maidstone Utd.
| Luton Town v. Watford.

UNITED LEAGUE.

Watford v. Luton.

LONDON LEAGUE.

Clapton Orient v. Queen's Park Rangers. | Tottenham Hotspur v. Woolwich Arsenal.

SCOTTISH LEAGUE.

Aberdeen v. Kilmarnock. | Heart of Midlothian v.
Partick Thistle v. Falkirk. | Motherwell.
Dundee v. Greenock Morton. | Celtic v. Hibernians.
Queen's Park v. St. Mirrens. | Port Glasgow v. Third
Airdrieonians v. Glasgow R. | Lanark.

OTHER MATCHES.

Clapton v. Townley Park. | Ipswich Town v. New
Yeovil Casuals v. Upton Pk. | Crusaders.

NORTHERN UNION.

Keighley v. Bradford. | Dewsbury v. Huddersfield.
Halifax v. Batley. | Salford v. Hull.
Hunslet v. Bramley. | York v. Leeds.
Brighouse R. v. Normanton. | Warrington v. Leigh.
Broughton R. v. Wigan. | St. Helens v. Millom.
Wakefield Trinity v. Castleford. | Morecambe v. Oldham.
| Rochdale Hornets v. Swint'n

LEAGUE CLUBS' PROSPECTS.

To-day's matches include the inter-League international between England and Scotland at Middlesbrough and the amateur international between England and Wales at Bishop Auckland. Strong teams will turn out in both these matches, and it is quite reasonable to anticipate the success of England in both encounters.

Considerable progress will also be made in the minor cup competitions all over the country, but there is nothing of outstanding interest in the way of senior cup competitions. In the big leagues, however, some interesting games are promised.

Blackburn Rovers, the leaders of the First League, visit Birmingham to play the Villa. A few weeks ago this would have been a very difficult task for the Rovers, but the Villa have suffered much from injuries to players and not a little from insubordination in their ranks. Their defence is weak and the forwards are not in their old-time brilliant form. So I expect Blackburn to at least hold their own.

Everton, who are second, should retain their place by winning at Oldham, and Newcastle United, although they have struck a rather bad patch of late, ought to beat Sunderland. Woolwich visit Bradford to play the City, and may be beaten, and the 'Spurs, who have not won a League match this year, will put a reorganised team in the field at Tottenham against Middlesbrough, in an attempt to secure a victory.

Sheffield Wednesday, on recent form, may beat Liverpool at Anfield. Bury, who visit Old Trafford to play Manchester United, will sustain their seventeenth defeat; Preston North End, if they maintain their recent good form, may beat Notts County; Bolton Wanderers ought to beat Manchester City; and Sheffield United should account for West Bromwich Albion.

Positions are continually changing in the Second League. Chelsea got there last Saturday through the defeat of Derby County at Glossop, but during the week Burnley have beaten Barnsley, and now claim a point advantage, but have played an extra match. Burnley, who are at home to Bradford, should retain the honour for another week at least. Chelsea have to visit Nottingham to play the Forest—never an easy task—and will do well to avoid defeat. Derby County, who have a match in hand of Chelsea and two of Burnley, should account for Hull at Derby, but Clapton, who are not without hopes of promotion, will have to be at their very best to win at Grimsby. A win there would put the East Enders on very good terms with themselves again.

Fulham have Barnsley for opponents at Craven Cottage, and should rake in the points. I am told that all hopes of securing a place in the First League are not yet abandoned in West London. Recent form such as last Saturday's victory at Hull, is good enough for anything. The other matches should be won by Leeds City, Leicester Fosse, Stockport County, Wolverhampton Wanderers, and Bristol City respectively.

The outstanding match in the Southern League this afternoon is at Brighton, where the local club have Plymouth as their visitors. It is bound to be a great contest, for the teams are well up in the table, and Plymouth have a possible chance of winning the championship. The surprise would not be great if they won.

Swindon, on their own ground, should beat Watford. The astonishing Reading team are at Northampton, and here we have two Cup teams engaged. Reading will be without that smart forward Bailey. The home team should win. Millwall should make no mistake against Brentford at New Cross, and Crystal Palace will have to go hard to win at Coventry.

Stoke, on their own ground, should have an easy time against Southampton, and West Ham will beat Exeter at Upton Park. Leyton, with the Rev. K. R. G. Hunt in their team, really ought to beat Norwich, but Leyton are so unreliable this season. Bristol Rovers look good for two points from New Brompton. Luton will make Queen's Park Rangers go all the way at Luton, but the Rangers, who are all out for the championship, should win.

P. J. M.

–LEGENDS–

Bill Davies

Bill Davies wrote his name into the record books at Palace when he became the club's first player to receive an international call-up, representing Wales in a 2-1 defeat by Scotland on 7th March 1908. Davies had two spells with the club and was a Palace player when he won his fourth and final cap. Only three players made more Southern League appearances for Palace than the Welshman, a versatile forward who spent most of his time playing wide on the left.

FOOTBALL –STATS–

Bill Davies

Name: Bill Davies

Born: November 1883 (Welshpool)

Died: 1960

Playing career: Shrewsbury Town, Stoke City, Crystal Palace, West Bromwich Albion, Crystal Palace; Wales

Position: Winger

Palace appearances: 207 (1907–08 and 1910–15)

Palace goals: 24

Wales appearances: 4

–LEGENDS–

Horace Colclough

FOOTBALL –STATS–

Horace Colclough

Name: Horace Colclough

Born: 7th November 1891 (Meir)

Died: March 1941

Playing career: Crewe Alexandra, Crystal Palace; England

Position: Left-back

Palace appearances: 85 (1912–15)

England appearances: 1

Horace Colclough joined Palace from Crewe Alexandra in the summer of 1912 and proved a superb acquisition. His form at full-back, mainly on the left, endeared him to fans of the club and also to those in the corridors of power at the FA. Thus Colclough became the first Crystal Palace player to receive an England call-up, and he won his first and only cap in 1914, a game against Wales on 16th March which the Three Lions won 2-0. A leg injury sustained in the First World War – reports of how it happened vary, but among them are claims that he was injured playing in a game for the army and others which say he suffered a gunshot wound – cut short Colclough's career and in August 1920 he was appointed first-team coach at Dutch side Heracles Almelo. During his time in Holland, he was dubbed "d'n trainer met ne poot genoemd" – the trainer with *that* leg.

LEFT: Colclough's performance in a 1-0 victory over Woolwich Arsenal in the Kent Cup on 16th October 1912 merited special mention in the following day's *Mirror*.

PALACE BEAT THE ARSENAL.

After a capital game Crystal Palace beat Woolwich Arsenal by 1 goal to 0 in the Kent Shield at Sydenham yesterday. The weather was dull and rain fell in the second half. There were 4,000 spectators. The Arsenal were without several of their regular players, and the Palace lacked the services of Collyer, Hughes and Smith. Early in the game Crawford, the Arsenal goalkeeper, stopped a penalty taken by Bulcock. Palace had all the best of the game, but were weak in front of goal, and at half-time there was no score. The Palace were the better team subsequently. Davies scoring for them five minutes before the finish.

It is quite likely that had the Crystal Palace team enjoyed the services of Smith, their regular centre forward, they would have won by a much greater margin. Chance after chance was given the inside men, chiefly by Davies, the outside left, but all went begging.

One of the best features of the game was the excellent display given by Colclough, the reserve right full-back of the Palace. Very quick on his feet, he frequently dashed in and got to the ball when failure seemed certain. His tackling was quite sound, and he kicked admirably. Altogether Colclough compared most favourably with his famous colleague, Bulcock, in a team which was strong both in defence and attack.

With players including captain George Woodger, Jimmy 'Ginger' Williams, George Payne and Harry Hangar, Palace continued to grow as a club and in the 1910–11 season, despite losing Woodger, the Glaziers finished fourth in Southern League Division One. Centre-forward Woodger was an outstanding player – he went on to be capped by England – and was snapped up by Oldham, of Division One, on 30th September 1910 for a fee of £800. Local lad Woodger, nicknamed 'Lady' by fans, was replaced by Charlie Woodhouse but, tragically, Woodhouse died suddenly a year later, during the 1911–12 season. Ted Smith duly arrived from Hull City and went on to score 124 senior goals for the club before the start of the First World War. Smith's first game for Palace was at West Ham United on 30th December 1911, a game in which both he and Dick Harker struck hat-tricks as the visitors won 6-1.

On Monday 17th November 1913, the *Mirror* carried a picture of Ted Smith scoring Palace's third goal in a stunning 5-1 victory over Reading two days earlier. Smith had struck twice, with Bill Davies, Percy Keene and Charles Hewitt also on the scoresheet for the home side.

Josh Johnson, the Palace goalkeeper from 1908 to 1915, was pictured in action against West Ham in the *Mirror* on 2nd February 1914. Despite Johnson's best efforts, the Glaziers were beaten 2-0 in the FA Cup second-round tie by their London rivals.

Flying the Nest
1918-1939

Joe Nixon, left, spent six years at the club between 1921 and 1927 but made just 31 appearances and scored one goal. The man standing next to him in this lovely pre-season snap, however, was an imposing defender and first-team regular who arrived at Palace from the Coldstream Guards. Centre-half Jimmy Hamilton made 196 appearances for the club between 1923 and 1931, scoring five goals.

1918 The end of the First World War marked the dawn of a new era in Britain and also in the club's history. Palace moved to a new stadium in Selhurst called The Nest, stepping in and leasing it from the London, Brighton & South Coast Railway Company after Croydon Common, its original inhabitants, folded. Palace got off to a flier at the start of the 1918–19 season, beating Queens Park Rangers 4-2 in the London Combination on 14th September in their first game at their new home. **1920–21** Palace lifted the inaugural Division Three crown and secured promotion to Division Two. **1924–25** The club were on the move again, this time to a purpose-built stadium by the name of Selhurst Park. Their first match there was against Sheffield Wednesday on 30th August. It ended in defeat and set the tone for the season, with Palace finishing 21st and suffering relegation. **1925–26** Manager Edmund Goodman steps down in November and is replaced by Alex Maley. **1927–28** Maley leaves the club in October and is replaced by Fred Mavin about five weeks later. **1930–31** In October, Jack Tresadern takes over from Mavin and leads the club to second place, thanks in no small part to the goals of Peter Simpson. He scores 46 goals in 42 games to set a new record for most League goals in a season. **1935–36** Tom Bromilow replaces Tresadern. **1936–37** RS Moyes is appointed as manager ahead of the new season, but leaves in December. Bromilow returns in January 1937. **1939–40** Palace remain in Division Three (South) as the Second World War breaks out, despite finishing second on three occasions. As war rages, Palace, now under another new manager in George Irwin, played in a number of competitions, including the South Regional League, London League and Football League South.

An enormous crowd witnessed the semi-final match for the London Victory Cup between Chelsea and Crystal Palace at Highbury.—(Daily Mirror photograph.)

LEFT As the caption which accompanied this picture in the *Mirror* on 21st April 1919 confirmed, a huge throng descended on Highbury to watch London rivals Palace and Chelsea clash in the London Victory Cup. Palace had beaten Brentford 1-0 thanks to a goal from Alan Stephenson on 17th February, but were thrashed 4-0 in this game.

Huge changes were afoot at Palace and in English football by the end of the First World War, not least with the club moving to a new ground called The Nest in 1918 and, ahead of the 1920–21 campaign, the Southern League Division One becoming Division Three of the Football League. The Glaziers, still under manager Edmund Goodman, won 24 and drew 11 of their 42 matches that season to win Division Three by five points from Southampton and gain promotion to Division Two. Wing-half Roy McCracken's call-up by Northern Ireland meant he became the first international player from Division Three. Another player whose contribution greatly helped Palace to the title that season was John Conner, the little forward who scored 29 League goals.

ABOVE: On 8th April 1921, the *Mirror* carried this picture of action from Palace's London Combination game against Chelsea which took place the previous day. Jack Alderson was the regular first-choice goalkeeper but George Irwin, who would go on to manage Palace, arrived and proved an able deputy.

ABOVE & LEFT: Everton were destroyed 6-0 in the first round of the FA Cup on 7th January 1922 and the *Mirror* recorded the result with a sequence of pictures. Bert Menlove and John 'Jack' Conner scored two goals apiece, with John Whibley and Alan Wood also registering for Palace.

RIGHT: Jack Alderson is captured in action during a 1-1 draw with Hull City on Humberside on 14th October 1922 and this picture appeared in the *Mirror* two days later. Joe Nixon scored for Palace that day. The two sides had also fought out a 1-1 draw a week earlier – home and away fixtures were back to back, more often than not that season – with Norman Waite scoring in London. Alderson won just one cap for England, in a 4-1 victory over France in May 1923.

> " *We went to Goodison Park and we whipped Everton by six goals to none. In Croydon they blinked when they read what had happened, and a story got about that one of the directors, who had been down with 'flu, was a cured man when the news came through on the Saturday evening.* "
>
> Bert Menlove

Palace remained in Division Two for four seasons and found themselves mixing it with some of the biggest names in the English game. Wolverhampton Wanderers, Derby County, Notts County, Leeds United and – oh, of course – Manchester United, were all opponents during their stay. There was another move of stadium as the club relocated to Selhurst Park, the ground they still call home today, ahead of the 1924–25 season, although the first League game at the new stadium, on Saturday 30th August 1924, was marked with a 1-0 defeat by Sheffield Wednesday. Sadly, that was a sign of things to come that season and, with only Coventry City finishing below Palace, the club were relegated to Division Three (South). That marked the beginning of the end for long-serving manager Edmund Goodman, who stepped down after 749 League games in charge at the end of November 1925. Goodman, who was replaced by Alex Maley, continued in his role as club secretary.

ABOVE: Jack Alderson gets a good punch clear while under pressure against Notts County on 2nd February 1924 in the second round of the FA Cup at The Nest. The game ended 0-0, as did the replay after extra-time. As did the second replay after extra-time. There really wasn't much to separate the two sides but, thankfully, the third replay, on 18th February, did just that with Palace winning 2-1. Tom Hoddinott and Bill Hand scored the goals.

LEFT: A lovely photo which appeared in the Mirror on 15th December 1927 didn't record a good result for Palace – a 2-1 defeat by Swindon in a second-round replay in the FA Cup the previous night – but it did capture Selhurst Park in full working glory. Palace, for whom Henry Hopkins had scored, had moved into the stadium three years earlier.

Smart Alex

Scot Alex Maley only oversaw one full season at Palace. After taking over from Edmund Goodman, he steered the team to a mid-table finish and the following campaign, 1926–27, led them to a respectable sixth, albeit with a points tally of 45, which was a long way short of champions Bristol City's 62. He lasted only until October 1927 and Fred Mavin, a month later, took over. Mavin, however, couldn't get Palace out of Division Three (South) either, although he was seriously unlucky not to. In the 1928–29 season he led his side to second place behind Charlton Athletic, level with them on 54 points but slipping behind on goal difference. It was the closest he would come and, on 18th October 1930, he parted company with the Glaziers. Two goals apiece from Albert Harry and George Clarke, and one from Peter Simpson, gave the club a 5-2 League victory over Fulham that day.

A month earlier, on 19th September, there had been sad news for all at Palace when highly respected chairman Sydney Bourne had passed away, although the club made sure they gave him a send-off he'd have been proud of by recording a thumping win against Newport County the day after his death. Simpson scored a hat-trick, and further goals from Hubert Butler, Harry Havelock, Harry and Clarke saw the game end 7-1. Simpson was on fire in front of goal that season, scoring 46 times, and Jack Tresadern led Palace to second in the table behind Notts County.

Alex Maley had the unenviable task of replacing Edmund Goodman, Palace's manager for 18 years, when he took over in November 1925.

Bobby Greener was a Crystal Palace player between 1921 and 1932, and made 317 appearances for the club. He scored six goals in that time.

The Team That Jack Built

Jack Tresadern remained in charge until June 1935, when he left the club to take over at Tottenham Hotspur. Tom Bromilow took charge at Palace for a season and was then replaced by RS Moyes, but Bromilow returned in January 1937.

Poor old manager Jack Tresadern's luck wasn't always in on the injury front, as these two *Mirror* cuttings prove.

On 9th November 1933, the paper recorded the plight of his stricken team ahead of a clash with Brighton & Hove Albion and, little more than a year later, the Palace boss was in the wars himself.

BAD LUCK FOR THE PALACE

Captain and Left-Half Strain Muscles at Practice

A stroke of bad luck makes it impossible for Jack Tresadern, manager of Crystal Palace, to select his team to meet Brighton at Selhurst on Saturday until the day before the game.

Hayward, the club captain and right back, and Smith, the new left half, who has been in brilliant form for the Palace, both strained leg muscles during ball practice.

They are very doubtful starters, and to add to this trouble, Rossiter, a reserve back, is suffering from an ankle injury.

Fourteen Fulham players, with Mr. J. H. McIntyre, the manager, left London yesterday for Teignmouth, where they will rest until Saturday, when they meet Plymouth Argyle.

Keeping, who has a strained leg muscle, is with the party, but if he is not fit his place at left back will be filled by Tilford.

It is possible that there will be a change in the forward line, as Wood and Richards have been asked to travel.

BRENTFORD—NO CHANGE ?

Brentford are hoping to play an unchanged team against Bradford City at Griffin Park on Saturday.

The only doubt is Astley, who was injured at Blackpool and who left after the game to be married at Dublin. No deputy has yet been decided on if Astley cannot play.

Mills, the Clapton Orient forward, who did so well when playing for Wales in his first international game last Saturday, will be in his usual place at inside left for the match against Exeter City at Exeter.

The team has not been definitely chosen, but there may be a change or two from the eleven that defeated Gillingham.

MILLWALL'S CHOSEN

Millwall's team to meet Bradford at Bradford on Saturday next will be:

Yuill; Sweetman, Walsh; Swallow, Hancock, Forsyth; Horton, Alexander, Bond, Ranson, Fishlock.

Wilson and Roberts have been X-rayed for foot injuries. The former has no bones broken, but is not yet fit, while Roberts has torn a lateral ligament, which will need a period of rest.

Graham and Newcomb are only recovering slowly from their recent injuries.

MANAGERS ON SICK LIST

Mr. Jack Tresadern, the Crystal Palace manager, who broke his leg recently, is back in harness at Selhurst Park.

Mr. James Hogan, the Fulham manager, who is confined to bed, also hopes to be back at Craven Cottage this week.

ABOVE: Charlie Cross, left, played for Palace between 1922 and 1928, making 237 appearances for the club without ever scoring.

–LEGENDS–

Peter Simpson

Peter Simpson announced himself as a first-team player in spectacular fashion when, five games into the 1929–30 campaign, manager Fred Mavin gave him his chance. He took it superbly, bagging a debut hat-trick in a Third Division (South) game against Norwich City to secure a 3-2 win. It was a taste of what was to come from Simpson, who ended the season with 36 League goals to set a new club record. The following campaign he hit 46 League goals, a record which still stands. He also struck eight times in cup competitions to end the 1930–31 campaign with 54 goals in 48 games, the most goals scored in a season by a Palace player. His haul that season included four hat-tricks – the 19 trebles he scored for the club remains a record, too – and, thanks in no small part to Simpson's goals, Palace went unbeaten at home that season. Records were set left, right and centre by the sure-footed striker and it will come as no surprise to anyone that he remains Palace's all-time top scorer. Remarkably, he scored his 165 goals in 195 appearances.

FOOTBALL
–STATS–

Peter Simpson

Name: Peter Simpson

Born: 13th November 1904 (Leith)

Died: 14th March 1974

Playing career: Kettering, Crystal Palace, West Ham

Position: Striker

Palace appearances: 195 (1929–35)

Palace goals: 165

PALACE JUST SUCCEED

Played three, won three—such is the fine record of promotion-minded Crystal Palace, who won 2—1 despite the gallant effort of Coventry to stop the winning sequence at Selhurst Park.

Midway through the opening half, with the Palace a goal up, Coventry were awarded a penalty kick. Bourton, one of the deadliest sharpshooters in the game, took the kick, but he could do no better than bang the ball against the top of the crossbar.

The Palace served up splendid football to begin with, and fully deserved the goal which Norris bagged in the sixteenth minute.

Coventry, however, fought back gamely, and the clever scheming of Lauderdale led to a series of hot assaults on the Palace goal.

Just after the interval, however, Coventry were awarded another penalty, and this time Baker, their right half, made no mistake from the spot.

It looked any odds on a Coventry victory after that, for they appeared to be well on top. Peter Simpson, however, won the day for the Palace when, with five minutes to go, he pounced on a through pass from Roberts, swerved past Davison and fired the ball low to the corner of the net. That settled the issue.

Simpson, whose goal for the Palace with the last kick of the game spoilt the unbeaten record of Southend United at Selhurst on Saturday.

19

Byrne, Baby, Byrne

1940-1969

> "When you lose a player like Johnny [Byrne], you feel like you've lost half a team.

Johnny McNichol

When Was

21

1940–41 Palace follow up their march to the League South 'D' Division title by claiming the South Regional League crown this time out. **1941–42** The club play in the London League and the London War Cup, but return to the Football League South the following season. **1946–47** Palace return to Division Three (South). **1947–48** Jack Butler replaces Irwin as manager and Belgian Marcel Gaillard becomes the first player born outside of the British Isles to represent Palace when he plays in a 5-2 win over Watford. **1948–49** Palace finish bottom of Division Three (South) and Ronnie Rooke takes over as manager for the 1949–50 campaign. **1950–51** Rooke leaves the club at the end of November and is replaced by joint managers Fred Dawes and Charlie Slade. **1951–52** There is another change at the top when Dawes and Slade leave in October and are replaced by Laurie Scott. **1954–55** Scott lasts until October, when Cyril Spiers takes over. **1958–59** Division Four is formed and the club, now managed by George Smith, becomes a part of it. Arthur Wait takes over as chairman. **1959–60** George Smith is replaced by Arthur Rowe.
1960–61 Palace are runners-up in Division Four to secure promotion to Division Three. Johnny Byrne becomes the latest Palace star to earn international recognition for England. He represents his country against Northern Ireland at Wembley and joins a select band of players to win a Three Lions call-up while playing in the third tier of English football. **1962–63** Dick Graham takes over from Arthur Rowe in November. **1964** Palace finish second in Division Three to win promotion.
1965–66 Rowe returns as caretaker manager in January 1966 and is himself replaced in April that year when Bert Head is installed full-time. **1969** Palace are runners-up in Division Two and win promotion to the top flight for the first time in the club's history. Local boy Steve Kember is the man of the moment, scoring the winner against Fulham to seal their place in Division One.

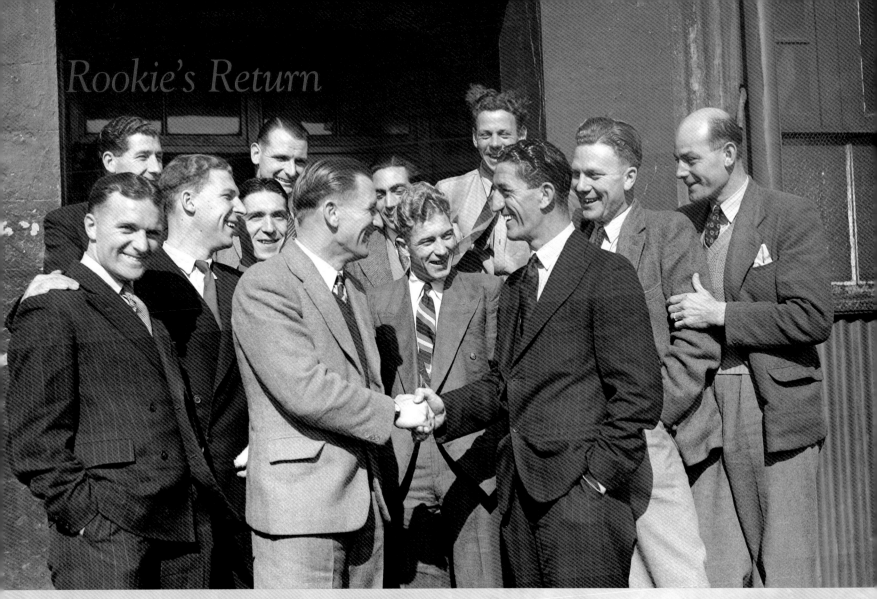

Rookie's Return

Former goalkeeper George Irwin became the club's first ex-player to be appointed manager when he took over in the summer of 1939, although his tenure would be dominated by the onset of the Second World War. Palace had played just three League games under Irwin when the war broke out and the Football League was suspended. Irwin remained in charge throughout the war years, with Palace operating in a number of different leagues before returning to Division Three (South) and, in 1947, he was replaced by Jack Butler. He had two seasons at the helm but left after the club finished bottom of the table. Another ex-player, centre-forward Ronnie Rooke, took over, returning to the club as player-manager and scoring 21 goals in 39 games in the 1949–50 season.

ABOVE: Crystal Palace players welcome new player-manager Ronnie Rooke back to Selhurst Park on 2nd May 1949. Rooke, a youngster at the club before the war, gets down to the less glamorous side of his job in his office later that day (inset).

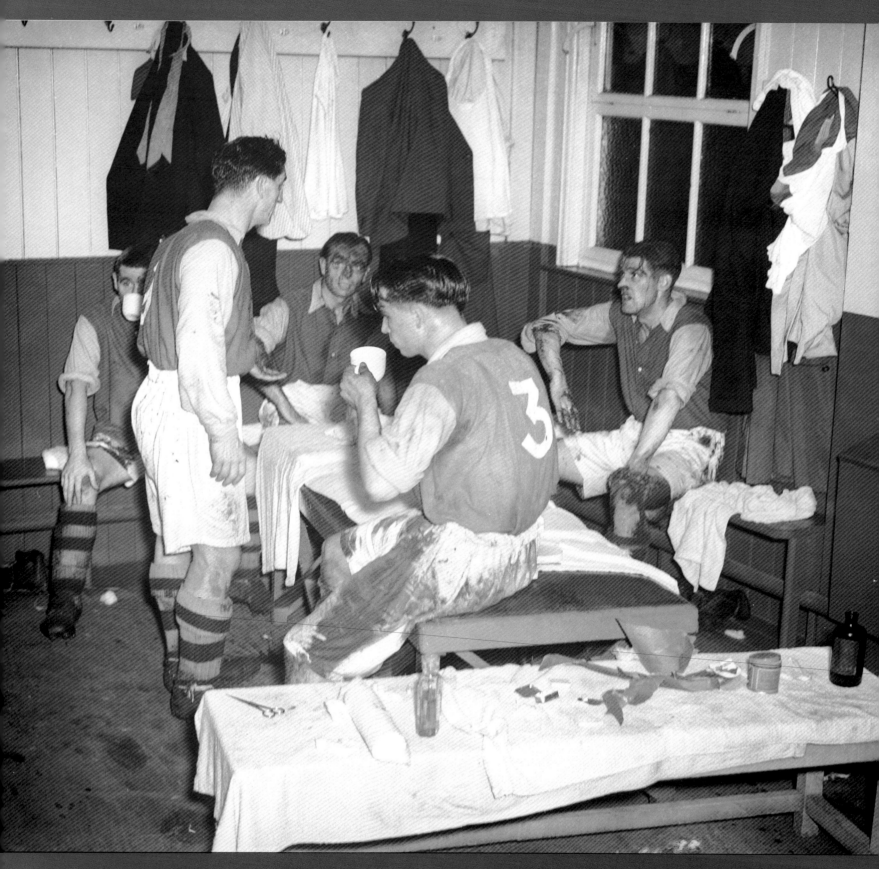

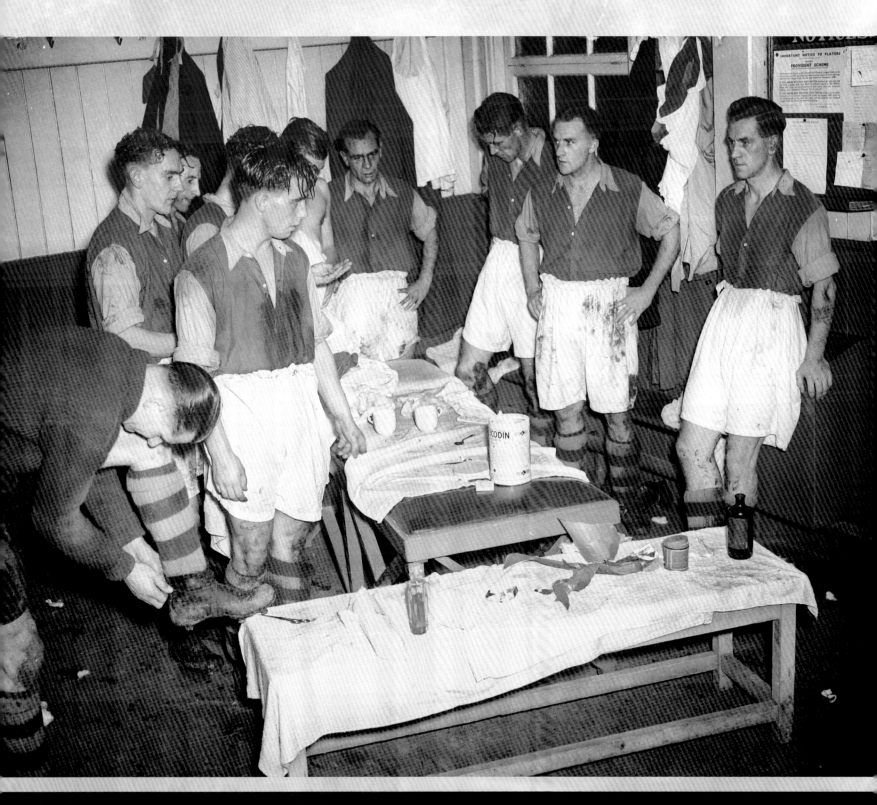

Palace players look as if they have been involved in a right old ding-dong in both of these shots . . . and they had. But what better way to recover from a tough first half than with a refreshing cup of tea? These pictures were taken at half-time during their FA Cup first-round clash with Newport County on 26th November 1949, a game Palace lost 3-0.

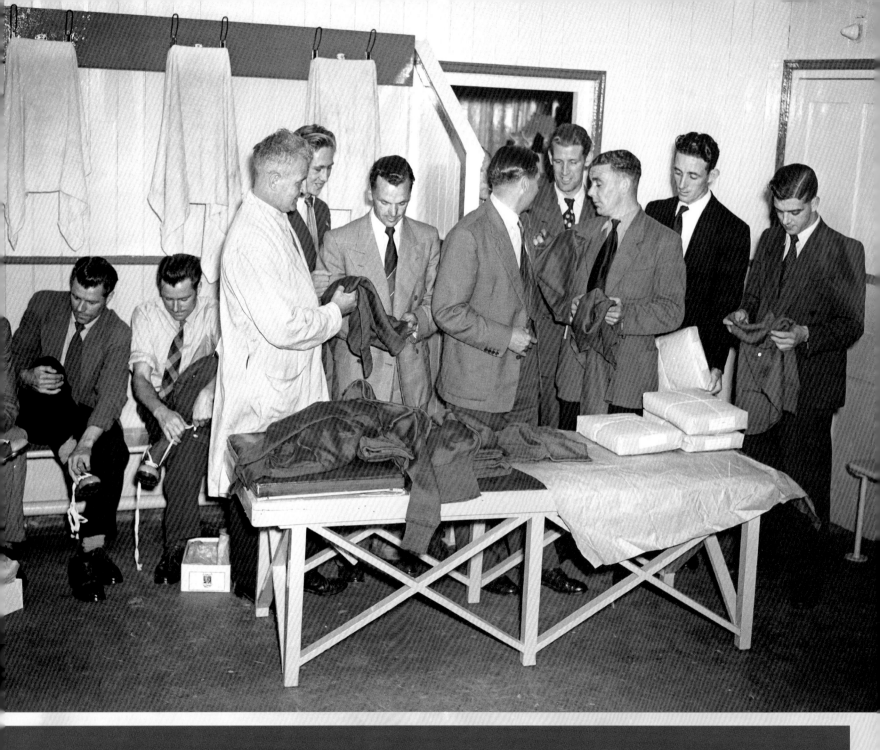

What's up, Doc? Thankfully, not a lot . . . well, not medically, at least. A meeting at the start of the 1950–51 season saw Palace players loaded up with new kit and a couple of them couldn't wait to try on their new boots. Perhaps they were just buying time before their medical assessments.

Ronnie Rooke only lasted one full season, guiding Palace to seventh in Division Three (South), and just four months into the 1951–52 campaign he was replaced by joint managers Fred Dawes and Charlie Slade. A lot had changed behind the scenes at Selhurst Park with a consortium of local businessmen, led by Arthur Wait, having taken ownership of the club.

RIGHT: Rooke entertains members of his playing staff as his squad assemble ahead of the new campaign.

The joint venture of Dawes, who had previously been assistant manager, and Slade, promoted from chief scout, lasted less than a year and, as the *Daily Mirror* reported the following October, Laurie Scott took charge. Full-back Scott joined the club as player-manager and played 20 games that season and eight the next before hanging up his boots. Palace had finished bottom under Dawes and Slade in the 1950–51 campaign, and only five teams finished below them the following season. Scott improved on that with a mid-table finish a year later, but, with the club third from bottom when the 1953–54 season ended and with a disappointing start to the next term, the poor showing ultimately led to his exit, with Cyril Spiers coming in as his replacement.

Joint managers are 'out'—as club bids for 'man to draw crowds'

By BOB FERRIER

LAURIE SCOTT, Arsenal and England full back, will spend his week-end contemplating a decision which might end his career as a player and set him off along the perilous path of football club management.

Crystal Palace have decided that Laurie is the man to give them a team and the success which will tap a vast South London potential, and fill their big stadium. They want him as a player-manager, but if Laurie is not happy about that, they want him as manager alone. Scott they are determined to have.

To clear the way for this, the club announced yesterday that the appointments of Fred Dawes and Charlie Slade, joint managers since Ronnie Rooke quit last December, have been "terminated." Slade goes back to his old post as chief scout to the club, and Dawes goes on twenty weeks' leave of absence with pay, a decision which, he said, "Comes as a shock to me."

If Laurie Scott goes to Palace as a player-manager, of course, Arsenal will demand a transfer fee in keeping with his football value, and I understand that the clubs are discussing this at the moment. Should he prefer to be manager only, Arsenal are likely to give him the Highbury blessing, and say nothing more than "Good luck, Laurie."

Although plagued by injuries in recent years, Scott has been a post-war pillar in the England defence, claiming seventeen full caps and more than thirty representative appearances for his country.

He is expected to give Crystal Palace a decision on Monday.

NEXT big item of football transfer news will be a move by Eddie Russell, the Wolves' wing half. Russell has not signed for Wolves for this season, and hasn't been seen around Molineux recently, but his absence from the Soccer scene has not gone unnoticed and you can expect Russell's transfer next week.

Into the Wolves team at home to Bolton go Gibbons, left back, from Ellesmere Port, home of his chief, Stan Cullis, and Deeley, right half, both getting their second League game. And Hancocks-sized Deeley faces up to Ray Parry, inside left, who at fifteen, becomes the youngest player to play in the First Division. Parry takes over from Harry Webster, having waited for a week to get his big chance.

Ray was set to go in against Sunderland last Saturday, but Webster's injured ribs were taped up, he played, and young Parry has waited impatiently this week for the news, 'Harry is unfit, you go in, son." from Bolton manager Bill Ridding.

LEFT: The *Mirror* reports the changes at the top on 13th October 1951, with Scott taking over from Dawes and Slade.

BELOW: Cyril Spiers' style of management sat very well with Frank Hearn, as he told the *Mirror* on 25th October 1954.

● Crystal Palace inside right Frank Hearn bubbled over with enthusiasm for the methods of new manager Cyril Spiers after the 3—1 win over Walsall. "He makes training a pleasure," says Frank. "And a daily spell of target practice makes all the difference to our shooting." Hearn hammered THAT point home with a thirty-yard goal.

Palace offer tennis star a try-out

By C. M. JONES

TENNIS star Roger Becker is rapidly making a name for himself in Soccer, too. Advised by his Davis Cup team-mate Geoffrey Paish to resume football as an antidote to staleness, Roger turned out two weeks running for a Croydon newspaper team.

Playing centre forward, he scored two goals on the first outing and five on the second, and has now been signed by Croydon Amateurs, the newly-formed Surrey Senior League club.

Their manager, the former Crystal Palace player Fred Dawes, will try Roger in the reserves tomorrow.

Roger's speed and fine positional sense have brought an invitation from Palace manager Laurie Scott to call in for a trial.

Whether or not Roger takes up this chance depends on his showing in senior amateur football.

LEFT: Dawes went on to manage Croydon Amateur, and he and Scott were both interested in a player called Roger Becker, the sort of bloke who annoys the rest of us mere mortals. As the *Mirror* reported on 23rd October 1953, Becker played tennis for Britain's Davis Cup team, but he was also a fine footballer, and his talent didn't escape the attentions of the two managers.

Palace goalkeeper Roy Bailey, whose son Gary would go on to become Manchester United's first-choice no. 1 during the 1980s, had a busy afternoon on 12th November 1955 when Leyton Orient stuffed the Glaziers 8-0 in a Division Three (South) fixture, and this picture shows him trying to thwart another effort from the visitors. It was a miserable campaign for Cyril Spiers' men, with only Swindon Town finishing below them. Their second-bottom finish meant Palace had to be re-elected into the Football League.

Palace stars line up for their pre-season photocall ahead of the 1957–58 campaign.

—LEGENDS—

Johnny Byrne

Johnny Byrne was 17 years old when he made his debut for Palace against Swindon in a 0-0 draw at Selhurst Park on Saturday 13th October 1956 and he would go on to become a real fans' favourite. Byrne finished the 1959–60 campaign as the club's leading scorer with 16 League goals and a year later he topped the charts again with 30. He was prolific and his goals helped the Glaziers, who scored 110 League goals that year under the management of Arthur Rowe, win promotion to Division Three as runners-up to Peterborough United. Byrne left for West Ham in March 1962 for a then-British transfer record fee of £65,000. He returned four years later and, by the time he left the club in 1968, had upped his haul to 90 League goals and 11 in the FA Cup.

RIGHT: The prolific striker was a real handful for defenders.

FOOTBALL —STATS—

Johnny Byrne

Name: Johnny Byrne

Born: 13th May 1939 (West Horsley)

Died: 27th October 1999

Playing career: Crystal Palace, West Ham, Crystal Palace, Fulham, Durban City (South Africa), Hellenic (South Africa); England

Position: Striker

Palace appearances: 259 (1956–62 and 1966–68)

Palace goals: 101

England appearances: 11

England goals: 8

Byrne and Bobby Charlton take instructions from England manager Walter Winterbottom at a practice match for the Three Lions against Fulham at Craven Cottage in August 1961. Byrne scored a hat-trick for England against the Portugal side, which featured Eusébio in a 4-3 win in May 1964.

Byrne served with the Royal Army Ordnance Corps during his time as a Palace player and is pictured here in full uniform in 1959.

Arthur Wait had been a Palace director for almost a decade when, in 1958, he became chairman and would remain in charge of the club for 14 years. Perhaps Wait's finest hour at the helm came on 18th April 1962 when he famously masterminded the visit of Real Madrid to Selhurst Park to mark the unveiling of the stadium's new floodlight system. Wait and his fellow power players at the club had wanted to invite a top northern side, but reportedly baulked at the sums they were asking. "If that's what they are going to do to us, we might as well try to get Real Madrid," he is claimed to have said. And, duly, he did.

Players lashed in programme
SENSATIONAL ATTACK AT PALACE

MIRROR SPORT REPORTER

A SENSATIONAL criticism of the Crystal Palace players by their manager George Smith appeared in last night's Palace programme.

Spectators at the game with Southport read a 1,000-word article by Mr. Smith critically summarising the team's performances.

ABOVE: Manager George Smith didn't hold back in his programme notes on 9th October 1958 and his criticisms could have arguably been aimed at the side at any time during that decade. Smith laid into his players ahead of the game against Southport, a 1-0 victory earned thanks to a goal from Tony Collins, after a disappointing start to the season and his words seemed to work. Things steadily picked up for Palace, who went on to finish the season in seventh place.

"The most disturbing fact to me is the inconsistency of effort," he wrote.

"On two occasions at least their performances as professional performers have been disgraceful.

"Yet on several occasions they have been praiseworthy — and in other matches like a patchwork quilt."

Forget

Mr. Smith said that early in the season he asked supporters to forget the past and support the players in their bid to redeem themselves. He went on:

"You have answered that nobly by the fact that our gates are much improved on last season.

"I cannot tell you how unhappy I am that we are not so far keeping our part of the bargain."

All the players knew of the programme contents before they went on the field.

After the match, which Palace won 1—0 with a goal by Tony Collins, Mr. Smith said:

"I am a bit happier than I was ninety minutes ago. But I still want more bite in front of goal."

Mirror Sport FIVE PAGES
Football With Forward... The Man Who Knows Them All

£20,000 TAG ON BYRNE

JOHNNY BYRNE, goal-grabbing, goal-making inside left, rocked Crystal Palace yesterday by suddenly asking for a move.

Palace granted his wish immediately—and set the transfer machinery in motion at Birmingham, Sunderland, Portsmouth and Wolves.

This dramatic decision by Byrne, 20, came forty-eight hours after he had hit two goals in the club's record 9—0 victory over Barrow.

It was a sad George Smith, manager of Palace, who spoke to me about his golden boy. He said:

"I tried to talk Johnny out of it. He was one of the lads I was building a team around.

"At the same time we felt that we could not stand in his way.

"I have no one on the books to replace him. That means I'll have to buy an inside forward.

"So whoever gets Byrne will have to start talking business at around £20,000."

Here is what Birmingham and Portsmouth had to say when they heard the news:

"I am definitely interested" — Pat Beasley, boss of Birmingham.

"You can count us among those who are keen" —Freddie Cox of Portsmouth.

Wolves have had Byrne, who was called up by the Army four months ago, watched frequently, while Alan Brown of Sunderland has been impressed by him.

So let battle commence for this former Palace ground-staff boy who is bound to set a record fee for the Fourth Division.

JOHNNY BYRNE
Four clubs interested

Palace golden boy is up for auction

end of last season. It takes place at Stamford Bridge tomorrow night.

But tonight Chelsea visit Brentford in the first round of the competition for 1959-1960.

So if they should lose the first game and win the next, they will be presented with a Cup that they have already LOST!

into our dressing-room and saw that both Trevor Smith and Neil had been cut by studs."

Eric Taylor, Wednesday's general manager, said last night: "We have no intention of making a special report on the match to the F.A."

Johnny Byrne shocked his manager George Smith when he demanded a transfer, as reported in the *Mirror* on 13th October 1959. Thankfully for Palace fans and despite interest from elsewhere, Byrne stayed put and it wasn't until an offer of £65,000 came in from Second Division West Ham United three years later that the goal-getting forward left the club.

Action from the final of the Southern Professional Floodlight Cup on 27th April 1959. Palace, at home, were beaten 2-1 by Arsenal, with Johnny Byrne scoring the Glaziers' goal.

The 1950s are not a time the club and its supporters look back on with particularly fond memories, and twice in that decade they were knocked out of the FA Cup by non-League opposition. A 1-0 defeat by Great Yarmouth on 27th November 1953 in the first round was followed a year later by a second-round exit at the hands of Bishop Auckland. Palace lost that game 4-2, with Len Choules and Bob Thomas scoring the consolation goals. The Glaziers did, however, fare much better against non-League opponents the night this picture was taken, recording a 3-0 victory over Margate in an FA Cup second-round replay on 9th December 1959. The two sides had drawn 0-0 at Margate four days earlier, but two goals from Johnny Roche and one from Alan Woan saw them safely through the rematch.

Palace fans join the players on the Selhurst Park turf to celebrate an FA Cup first-round victory over Portsmouth on 4th November 1961. The home side won 3-0, with one goal from Johnny Byrne and two from Ron Heckman.

Arthur Wait's Real Deal

The aforementioned visit of Spanish giants Real Madrid took place on 18th April 1962 to commemorate the opening of the new floodlighting system put in place at Selhurst Park by chairman Arthur Wait. Johnny Byrne, sold to West Ham for a British record fee of £65,000 a month earlier, returned to guest for the club against the original *Galacticos*. Hungary legend Ferenc Puskás and Argentina superstar Alfredo Di Stéfano wowed the home fans, although Palace put up a brave fight, eventually losing the game 4-3.

Action from the game against Real Madrid (left) shows Alfredo Di Stéfano heading at goal. During Real's stay in South London, Palace manager Arthur Rowe (above) caught up socially with Puskás (on his left) and Di Stéfano.

The aptly named Bill Glazier came through the ranks at Crystal Palace and on 13th January 1962 manager Arthur Rowe gave him his League debut in a Division Three clash at home to Halifax Town. This picture of Glazier was taken in August 1964, just two months before he was sold to Coventry for £35,000.

As the *Mirror* reported on 17th October 1964, the fee Coventry paid for Glazier was a then-British record for a goalkeeper. Glazier was only 21 at the time and the club replaced him with Wales international Tony Millington, whom they signed from West Bromwich Albion.

While the Fifties were largely nondescript for Palace, the Sixties were much more rewarding. The Glaziers finished second in Division Four in the 1960–61 season under Arthur Rowe and won promotion from Division Three in 1963–64 – now under the guidance of Dick Graham, another of the club's former goalkeepers – when they finished runners-up to Coventry City. This picture was taken on 25th April 1964 as the club celebrated that promotion despite losing their final game of the season 3-1 to Oldham Athletic. A penalty from Cliff Holton gave Palace their goal that day.

Palace had a home game in Division Two scheduled for Wednesday 15th March 1965 and it looked in doubt two days earlier when snow covered Selhurst Park. However, players and staff came together to clear the pitch and the terraces, and they were rewarded with a 1-0 victory over Preston North End courtesy of a Cliff Holton goal.

Head, Coach

Bert Head was appointed manager in April 1966 by chairman Arthur Wait, taking over from Dick Graham, and three years into his reign he would become the first manager to lead Palace into the top flight. The club finished seventh in Division Two in Head's first season in charge and 11th a year later, but in the 1968–69 season they finished runners-up to Brian Clough's Derby County to win promotion. He would remain at the helm for seven years.

RIGHT: Head ponders the way to beat Manchester United in Crystal Palace's top-flight debut. This picture was taken on 8th August 1969, the day before the game at Selhurst Park.

Head looks on from the dugout as Palace beat Portsmouth 3-1 on 5th April 1969. John Sewell (from the penalty spot), Steve Kember and Cliff Jackson got the goals that day.

Palace line up pre-match in November 1966. Back row, from left to right: Barry Dyson, Jack Bannister, Bobby Woodruff, John Jackson, David Payne, Alan Stephenson, Bert Howe. Front row: Cliff Jackson, Brian Wood, Terry Long, Steve Kember.

–LEGENDS–

Steve Kember

Another local lad, Croydon-born Steve Kember came through the ranks at Palace and etched his name into club folklore at the end of the 1968–69 season when he scored the winning goal in the crucial clash with Fulham which took Palace into the top flight for the first time in the club's history. Kember captained the club for a short time towards the end of his first spell but, by the time he returned, Palace's fortunes had dipped and they were back in Division Two. The tough-tackling midfielder soon made an impact on the club for a second time though, and helped them win promotion back to the top flight at the end of the 1978–79 campaign. Kember was sold to Vancouver Whitecaps a year later but, after 12 months in Canada, he returned home and chairman Ron Noades put him in charge of Palace's youth set-up. When Dario Gradi was sacked, Kember was handed the manager's job for the first time, and he would take charge four times in total, twice full-time and twice as a caretaker. Kember's long association with Palace means he remains a hugely popular figure at the club today.

FOOTBALL –STATS–

Steve Kember

Name: Steve Kember

Born: 8th September 1948 (Croydon)

Playing career: Crystal Palace, Chelsea, Leicester City, Crystal Palace, Vancouver Whitecaps (Canada)

Position: Midfielder

Palace appearances: 291 (1965–71 and 1978–80)

Palace goals: 38

ABOVE: Kember signs an autograph for a young fan ahead of a cricket match against Wallington in Surrey on 11th July 1971.

LEFT: No shin-pads required for Steve Kember as he lays the ball off before Manchester United's Alan Gowling can get to him during a 3-1 defeat at Selhurst on 11th September 1971. Mel Blyth scored Palace's goal.

BELOW: A youthful Kember slides in to tackle Millwall player Tom Wilson on 15th October 1966. The game at The Den ended 1-1, with Barry Dyson scoring for the visitors.

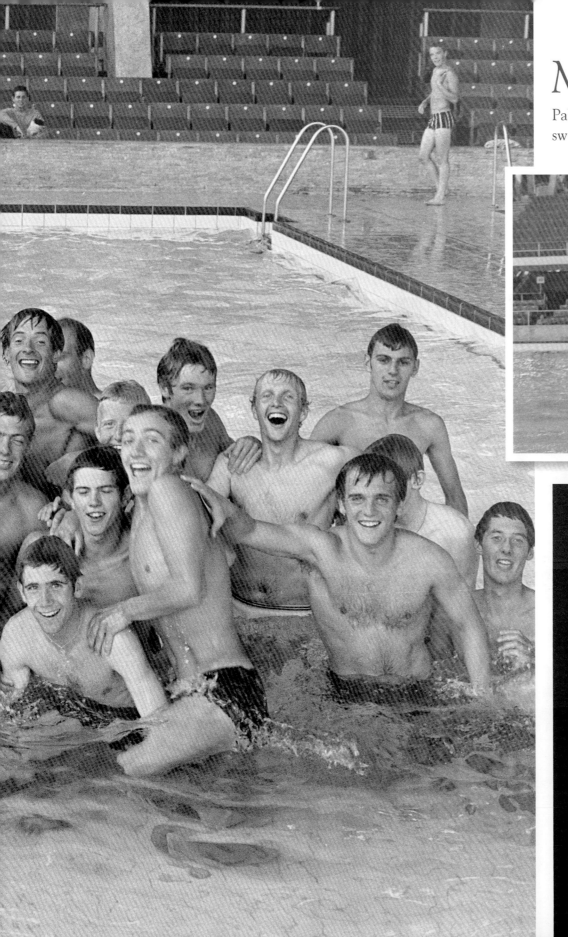

Making a Splash

Palace stars lark about at Crystal Palace swimming baths on 18th July 1967.

A month later and all dried off, Palace stars report for their pre-season photocall.

The 1968–69 season began in style for Bert Head's men with a 4-0 victory over Cardiff at Ninian Park which set the tone for the rest of the campaign. David Payne and Mel Blyth scored a goal apiece, and Cliff Jackson struck twice to sink the Bluebirds.

Palace keeper John Jackson gathers a shot from Cardiff striker John Toshack in the victory on Saturday 10th August 1968.

LEFT Incredibly, John Sewell was never booked in a career which saw him make more than 200 Football League appearances for both Charlton Athletic and Palace. The right-back was handed the captain's armband at Selhurst Park in the 1967–68 season and led the club to promotion to Division One the following year. He eventually left Palace in 1971, bound for Leyton Orient, having made 258 appearances and scored nine goals. Six of those came in the League and the majority of them from the penalty spot.

Mark Lazarus joined Palace from Queens Park Rangers mid-way through the 1967–68 season and played a major role in the promotion-winning campaign which followed. However, he only played four times in the top flight before manager Bert Head sold him to Leyton Orient.

Palace were there or thereabouts throughout the 1968–69 campaign, as were the Derby County side of Brian Clough, and both meetings between the two teams – at the Baseball Ground on 30th November and Selhurst Park on 5th March – received plenty of newspaper coverage. Steve Kember sponges off the sweat after training ahead of that first encounter while John Sewell speaks to a reporter to preview the return fixture. Derby, third at the time, won their home game 2-1, with John McCormick scoring Palace's consolation goal, although it was a different story back in South London as the runners and riders in the race for promotion began to turn for home. Derby topped the table that day but it was Palace who won the fixture 1-0 in front of a crowd of 31,748. The goal from Bobby Woodruff gave their promotion hopes a real shot in the arm and the fans a belief that something special was starting to happen.

PAGE 30 DAILY MIRROR, Thursday, March 20, 1969

Going up?

PALACE ON THE BRINK

CUP PITCH IS 'A VAST SOGGY MESS'

By PETER INGALL

THE FA CUP semi-final between Leicester and the holders West Bromwich Albion is likely to be postponed for seven days because the Hillsborough pitch is virtually unplayable.

This was the gloomy forecast from Sheffield last night, and the game is expected to be called off after a 10 a.m. inspection today.

The Hillsborough pitch —home of Sheffield Wednesday—was yesterday described as "a vast soggy mess" following the snow, sleet, and rain which has hit the area in the last week.

Sheffield Wednesday general manager Eric Taylor said last night: "Winter must turn into spring overnight to give us a chance of getting the pitch ready. At the moment it looks something like a huge black blancmange."

Both clubs turned down a suggestion that the semi-final should be played next Wednesday because they felt it was unfair to ask their supporters to travel for a night match.

So after it was agreed that the tie would be put back a week, the Football League gave both clubs permission to arrange important League games on Saturday.

Leicester will visit Southampton and Albion bring forward their fixture at Nottingham Forest.

By KEN JONES: Crystal Palace 4, Millwall 2

GEARED to the vigour and tension of a South London promotion clash, Crystal Palace found themselves playing only half a match against Millwall last night.

It was enough to stretch the nerve ends of their supporters and threaten the decimal-point difference which now nudges Palace into second place behind Derby in the Second Division.

Their fifth successive win makes them clear contenders for a place in the First Division next season.

But the errors Palace committed as Millwall staged a second-half revival will bear thinking about if they eventually make it.

Seven minutes from time Palace were lying third in the promotion race, struggling to recover their rhythm in the face of Millwall's fight back.

But a goal scrambled through a ruck of Millwall defenders by centre forward Bobby Woodruff sent those with statisticians' minds scurrying over their figures.

Palace were indeed second. But they had more than mathematics on their mind in a fiercely contested second half which began with Millwall trailing by three goals.

Antics

Until then it had seemed as though only referee Roger Kirkpatrick had read anything more than average issues into what had threatened to be a fierce and thrilling battle.

His antics served to irritate players who, prepared to give every ounce of endeavour, still stayed on the side of legality.

Palace moved comfortably forward after the twenty-second minute when a cleverly taken free-kick gave Colin Taylor the chance to fire left-footed past Millwall goalkeeper Bryan King.

They got a second when Millwall, with more than enough men to cover at a corner, allowed Palace centre half John McCormick a chance he took eagerly close in.

A linesman was flagging but with no one to notice him Palace acclaimed what looked like a comfortable and winning lead.

Although Millwall launched occasional threatening raids through Gordon Bolland and Derek Possee, they too often left forwards to hunt without support. Spaces in midfield, where the ball could be worked went ignored.

It looked even easier for

TOP PLACES

	P	W	D	L	F	A	Pts
Derby	34	18	11	5	65	36	47
Palace	35	18	7	9	58	40	43
Cardiff	35	18	5	11	62	45	43
Middlesbrough	34	18	7	9	60	37	43
Millwall	35	17	7	11	55	46	41
Charlton	35	14	11	9	47	44	39

Woodruff puts them second in battle of decimals

Palace, a minute before half-time when Mark Lazarus freed the ball from Millwall's defenders and sent it on for Woodruff to score with ease.

Millwall started the second half with Barry Salvage deputising for the injured Billy Neil and the appearance of such a name suddenly seemed symbolic of Millwall's prospects.

Possee's sharp finish after good play on Palace's left by Bolland and Keith Weller awoke Millwall to the possibility of saving the match.

McCormick's tragic own goal strengthened that belief as Millwall came eagerly forward.

But, although their fight back was brave and in the end Palace knew they had been in a match, it was not enough to keep the promotion hopes of both clubs alive.

The *Mirror* charted Palace's bid to go up every step of the way. On 5th April 1969, reporter Harry Miller's words recorded a 0-0 draw at home to Middlesbrough as the race for the top two spots began to hot up and, a week later, Miller was told by manager Bert Head that two more points ought to guarantee promotion. Palace were at Preston North End's Deepdale that day and fought out a 0-0 draw, meaning that with two games to go – against Fulham at home and Blackburn Rovers at Ewood Park – they still needed at least a point to go up.

RECORD CROWD GETS A SOCCER SHUT-OUT

Two booked in Palace crunch

By HARRY MILLER   Crystal Palace 0, Middlesbrough 0

CRYSTAL PALACE closed the gates on their best-ever League crowd yesterday—then experienced a Soccer shut-out that does nothing to solve the Second Division promotion puzzle.

A tough, tension-ridden match without a goal provided little entertainment for 43,381 fans. But as Palace boss Bert Head said later:

"Both sides have worked for nine months to get within sight of the First Division. They weren't going to throw the chance away in one game."

It was tough all right. Two players were booked in the second half—Palace's Roger Hoy, and Middlesbrough schemer Johnny Crossan.

Hoy foiled Crossan with a late tackle, and Crossan retaliated.

Middlesbrough left Selhurst Park with a painful receipt for the point that keeps them heading for promotion as hopefully as Palace.

They had five injured players under treatment last night—and two are unlikely to be fit for another vital clash, against Charlton, this afternoon.

Manager Stan Anderson told me: "Crossan and David Chadwick have knee injuries and must be rated doubtful. The others should be all right.

Tight

"I'm satisfied with a draw today. We came here to win, but Palace played it so hard and tight that we didn't have much scope to attack them."

Middlesbrough, with Alec Smith, Eric McMordie and Crossan outstanding, looked the better organised side in a match dominated by muscle rather than skill.

Palace had their best chance of winning in the seventh minute, when Mark Lazarus hit a shot that goalkeeper Willie Whigham pushed up in the air and Gordon Jones headed clear as Cliff Jackson closed in.

Bryan King, Millwall goalkeeper, clutches in vain for Colin Taylor's shot that set Palace on the way to victory.   Picture: MONTE FRESCO

A Corker from Kember . . .

A 2-1 defeat by Blackpool at Selhurst Park on 25th January 1969, a game in which Steve Kember scored for Palace, had not been a good result, but little did everyone associated with the club know that day would be the last time they would have to deal with a loss in the League all season. The following League game, on 22nd February, saw the Glaziers record a 2-0 victory over Hull City, with goals from Mark Lazarus and John McCormick, and that result kick-started a 14-game unbeaten run which would take them to the brink of promotion with two games to play. Thankfully, they only needed one of those fixtures, the home clash against Fulham, and, with the Cottagers beaten 3-2, courtesy of goals from Mark Lazarus, Cliff Jackson and Steve Kember, second place and promotion were assured.

Steve Kember (main picture) celebrates a Palace goal and (below) wheels away in delight after scoring the third, vital goal.

Glaziers frontman Tony Taylor (below) puts pressure on Fulham goalkeeper Malcolm Webster.

. . . And a Proper Promotion Party to Follow

The victory over Fulham sparked some wonderful, emotional scenes at Selhurst Park with the players and fans in states of near-delirium. It had taken Palace 64 years but, finally, they could claim to be a Division One side.

John Jackson leads the celebrations (far left) as Bert Head's stars climb into the Selhurst stands to take the acclaim of the fans and there are souvenirs of the day for a lucky few as playing jerseys are tossed to the supporters. The celebrations went on long into the night, down on the pitch and back in the sanctuary of the dressing room . . . and most, although not all, were perfectly tasteful, too.

UP THE PALACE

LEFT & BELOW: Fans swarm the Selhurst Park pitch following the victory over Fulham.

–LEGENDS–

John Jackson

London-born John Jackson was handed his debut away at Swindon Town for what would be a 2-0 defeat on 25th August 1964, but from those inauspicious beginnings Jackson would go on to become a stalwart of the club and, in particular, the promotion-winning side. He was an ever-present in the League during the first three seasons in Division One and missed just four games during the fourth season in the top flight. A remarkable run in the team, which began on 19th August 1967 at Rotherham United's Millmoor, saw him make 254 consecutive appearances for Palace until 14th October 1972, when he missed an away game at Wolves. Jackson earned himself the nickname 'Stonewall' from those on the terraces of Selhurst Park.

RIGHT: Jackson lines up his wall during a 2-0 home defeat by Wolverhampton Wanderers on 18th March 1972.

FOOTBALL –STATS–

John Jackson

Name: John Jackson

Born: 5th September 1942 (Hammersmith)

Playing career: Crystal Palace, Leyton Orient, Millwall, Ipswich Town, Hereford United

Position: Goalkeeper

Palace appearances: 388 (1964–74)

The Palace keeper punches clear from Chelsea's Alan Birchenall in a 1-1 draw at Stamford Bridge on 30th August 1969. Roger Hoy got the Palace goal that day.

Posing at Selhurst Park on the day of the club's pre-season photocall in July 1972.

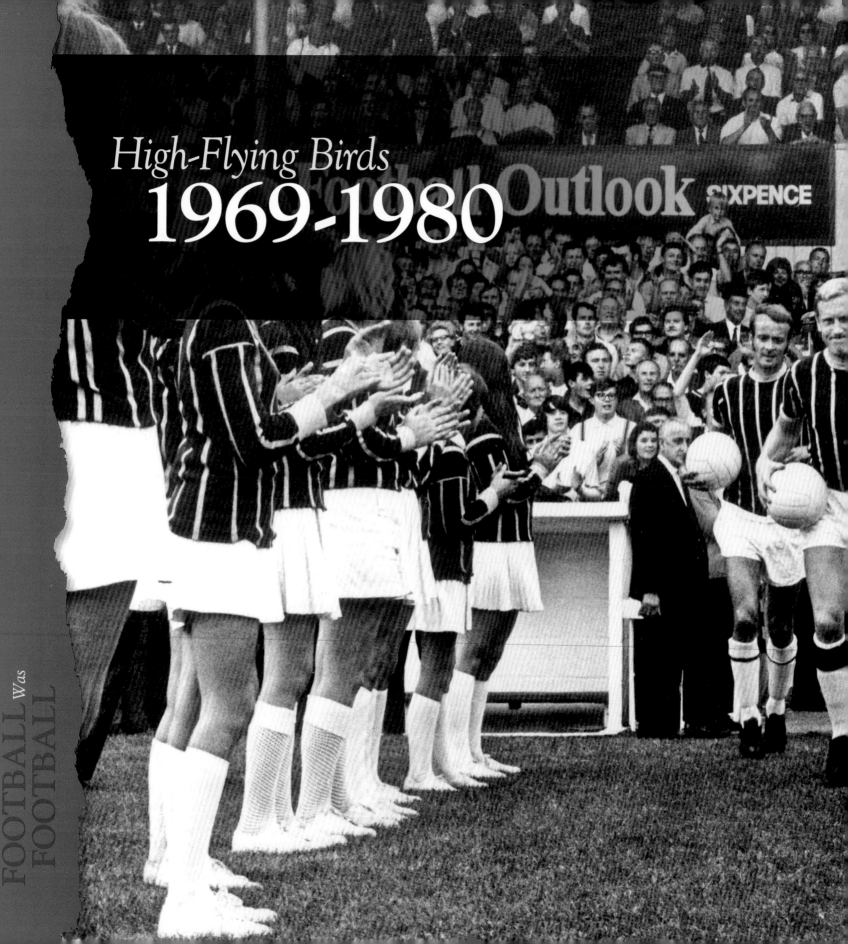

High-Flying Birds
1969-1980

John Sewell leads his Palace team-mates out through a guard of honour formed by the club's cheerleaders – the original Crystals – for their first Division One game, a home fixture against Manchester United on 9th August 1969.

1969–70 Palace play their first Division One fixture, a home game against Manchester United on 9th August. The game ends in a 2-2 draw. The club finishes third from bottom that season but it is enough to avoid the drop. **1970** Peter Wall, Bobby Tambling and Alan Birchenall join the club but a couple of household names, Cliff Jackson and Roger Hoy, depart. **1971** Ex-player George Petchey leaves his coaching position to take charge at Leyton Orient. Alan Birchenall and Steve Kember then leave just a month into the season as manager Bert Head shakes up his squad. **1972** Chairman Arthur Wait becomes life-president with Raymond Bloye taking over as chairman. Long-serving player Terry Long becomes assistant manager to Head. **1973** There are huge changes at Palace both in terms of history and personnel. In March, Malcolm Allison takes over the manager's hotseat and soon after the club changes its nickname and crest. Sadly, the stay in the top flight is over at the end of the 1972–73 season after four years and Palace slip back into Division Two. **1974** The club suffer back-to-back relegations and are demoted to Division Three. **1976** An unremarkable League campaign ends with Palace mid-table in Division Three, but a fine run to the semi-finals of the FA Cup gives the supporters some real excitement before eventual winners Southampton knock them out of the competition. In March that year, Peter Taylor follows Johnny Byrne by becoming the second Palace player to play for England while the club are in Division Three. **1977** Terry Venables takes over as manager and leads the club to promotion from Division Three. **1978–79** Palace return to the big time after winning the Division Two title. A record crowd of 51,801 turns out to see the Eagles play Burnley at Selhurst Park. **1980** Terry Venables leaves the club in October and Ernie Walley then Malcolm Allison take over for brief spells before the club is sold to Ron Noades early in 1981.

PALACE PLAN MOVE TO SUPER STADIUM

By NIGEL CLARKE

CRYSTAL PALACE are eager to move to an exciting new £5,000,000 ground at Croydon, built on the lines of Real Madrid's stadium.

Arthur Wait, chairman of newly-promoted Palace, said yesterday: "The new South London motorway has killed Selhurst Park."

The ring road, scheduled for 1974, will cut a large corner off Palace's present home. It will trim turnstiles, exits and toilets from the £180,000 Arthur Wait stand due to be completed in ten days.

The motorway has also had an inhibiting effect on Palace's plans for further ground developments at Selhurst.

"Six weeks ago we had planning approval for our improvements," explained chairman Wait. "Now we have heard the new road plan will take down what was approved.

"We had no idea. It

And there are flowers for the skipper's wife

IT'S GOING to be so friendly down at the Palace this season . . . well, before the match, at least.

Rival captains will receive a large bouquet of flowers for their wives, and there will be sherry in the dressing-room afterwards, plus a bowl of fruit.

Before each match, directors of opposing clubs will be entertained to a

was a shock, but this is progress. I don't foresee any alterations to the GLC's plan. It is one of the most finished blueprints ever produced. One would think that this is it.

"In the circumstances it would be ideal for us to move to the Croydon

meal, and the club presented with a silver wine tray.

Says manager Bert Head: "They are gestures we hope will not go unappreciated. The friendly touch before the ruthless business of playing football."

Palace have given Head the go-ahead to spend another £60,000 on two players before the start of the season on August 9.

Airport site. In fact, I would prefer it. The challenge of building a decent League football ground is tremendous.

"We envisage something like the Real Madrid set up. It would include every sporting facility.

"Of course we would

expect assistance from the local authorities and the GLC with this project. The cost I imagine would be something like £5,000,000.

"We could also give football fans what is desperately needed, the first forty-acre car park. That would really be something for Croydon. I'd love to do it.

"I don't believe in protests and demonstrations," added Wait, "If it's going to happen it will."

Palace will still press on with their new 7,000-seater double-decker stand at the Whitehorse Lane end of Selhurst Park. This part of their current development plan is scheduled to be finished in 1971-72.

LEFT: Palace's arrival in English football's big time came with some big ideas in the boardroom and manager's office as the club looked to impress. Chairman Arthur Wait was ready to leave Selhurst Park for a stadium along the lines of Real Madrid's Santiago Bernabeu and manager Bert Head introduced some classy touches which would make the directors and players of visiting teams most welcome in South London.

PALACE SET FOR £20,000 HYND MOVE

By NIGEL CLARKE

CRYSTAL PALACE yesterday agreed terms of around £20,000 for the transfer of Glasgow Rangers defender Roger Hynd—a nephew of Liverpool boss Bill Shankly.

Rangers manager Davie White will see Hynd this morning and the decision will then be left to the player, who was ill in bed yesterday while negotiations were going on

Search

If Hynd agrees to the move he is likely to slot into Palace's back four alongside centre half John McCormick.

Palace manager Bert Head leaves for a Spanish holiday on Saturday. When he returns, he will carry on the search for the extra two players he needs to equip his side for First Division football next season.

Tommy Craig, Aberdeen's 18-year-old midfield player, is expected to sign for Sheffield Wednesday today at a fee of around £100,000.

RIGHT: There was no end to the club's ambition after winning promotion to Division One and it was a case of "Next stop – Europe", as far as manager Head was concerned.

LEFT: *Mirror* football reporter Nigel Clarke reveals that a deal for Hynd is imminent on 6th May 1969.

Palace get ready for invasion of Europe

By NIGEL CLARKE

GO-AHEAD Crystal Palace are planning for European football at Selhurst Park in 1970.

Promoted Palace start their first-ever season in the First Division in just over two weeks' time on a big European bonus scheme.

These incentives have been written into the contracts of the first team squad, and manager Bert Head says: "I've told the players they have four ways of earning the money.

"They are the FA and League Cups, the League championship, and by finishing London's top club and getting into the Fairs Cup."

Head has no illusions about the fierce competition Palace will find in a League he describes as "the greatest in the world, and the most difficult to do well in."

Tough

He adds: "We have tried to leave no stone unturned. Of course it will be tough, but so far as playing is concerned that must be done by me.

"I will have to wait and see whether my players are good enough for the First Division, and whether it will be necessary to strengthen positions.

"We are all looking forward to the start, and are happy that five of our first seven matches are against Manchester United, Everton, Spurs, Liverpool and Chelsea."

It is a formidable challenge and Head joked: "We reckon if we can win the first ten games, we can take the title.

"Certainly we are not setting any other target at the start than two points a match."

Steve Kember, young Crystal Palace forward, takes a break from training in the sun yesterday.
Picture: MONTE FRESCO

Shopping for the Top Flight

Head chats with new signings (from left), Roger Hynd, Alan Pinkney and Gerry Queen in July 1969.

Manager Bert Head went on something of a recruitment drive in the summer of 1969 and snapped up Roger Hynd from Rangers, Alan Pinkney from Exeter City and Gerry Queen from Kilmarnock to boost his squad ahead of their first season in Division One. Players from Scotland often represented far better value for money than those purchased from clubs south of the border and Queen, in particular, would become a firm favourite with the Selhurst faithful.

Local lad David Payne came through the junior ranks at Palace and would go on to make 318 appearances for the club, many of which came in Division One, before following George Petchey to Leyton Orient.

Colin Taylor scored 10 goals for Palace in 40 appearances during the 1968–69 season, but was sold back to Walsall, from whom he had signed at the start of that campaign, in September 1969, just a month after this photograph was taken.

'After all this, the First Division will be almost a relaxation'

FANS GET PALACE TO PITCH ON TIME!

By KEN JONES

CRYSTAL PALACE launch themselves into the First Division against Manchester United today with the help of a final push from their fans.

Supporters volunteered to work late into the night to clear the debris of renovation which was still scattered around Selhurst Park at noon yesterday.

Manager Bert Head ... a summer of problems. Picture: MONTE FRESCO

The wait for life in the big time was finally over on 9th August 1969 and what better way to mark your arrival in Division One for the first time than a home game against the Manchester United of Bobby Charlton, George Best and Denis Law? It was a wonderful occasion at Selhurst Park with a record crowd of 48,610 creating a real party atmosphere, and a day which saw summer signings Gerry Queen and Roger Hynd make their debuts for the club. Mel Blyth would become the first Crystal Palace player to score in the top tier of English football when his header put the Londoners ahead and, even after Bobby Charlton had equalized, Palace's spirits didn't drop. Queen marked his debut with his first goal for the club to put Palace back into the lead before Willie Morgan bagged an equalizer. A 2-2 draw against United, which was shown on *Match of the Day*, was by no means a bad way to kick off life at the top table and would be the start of a season in which the club came up against some huge teams and plenty of famous faces from the era.

The Palace line-up against Manchester United for the club's first game in Division One was:

1. John Jackson.
2. John Sewell.
3. John Loughlan.
4. Roger Hoy.
5. John McCormick.
6. Roger Hynd.
7. Mark Lazarus.
8. Steve Kember.
9. Cliff Jackson.
10. Gerry Queen.
11. Mel Blyth.

Goalkeeper John Jackson pushes the ball clear from Denis Law in Palace's first Division One game, which ended 2-2.

Palace's promotion gave the fans a chance to watch some wonderful teams and individual talent at Selhurst Park, and there weren't many clubs bigger than Don Revie's Leeds United in the late Sixties. This match against the Yorkshiremen ended with another good result for Palace against a top side, a 1-1 draw in South London on 18th October 1969. Gerry Queen scored for the home side. (Main picture) Steve Kember battles for possession with Terry Yorath and (inset) Kember gets stuck in with Eddie Gray.

There weren't many tougher away trips than those to Stoke City's Victoria Ground, particularly on the back of two home defeats. Derby County, promoted with Palace that season, had enjoyed a 1-0 win at Selhurst Park and Coventry City had beaten Bert Head's side 3-0 before this fixture in the Potteries on 20th December 1969. It ended in yet another defeat, this time 1-0, as Palace embarked on a miserable run which wouldn't see them win again until 11th March 1970.

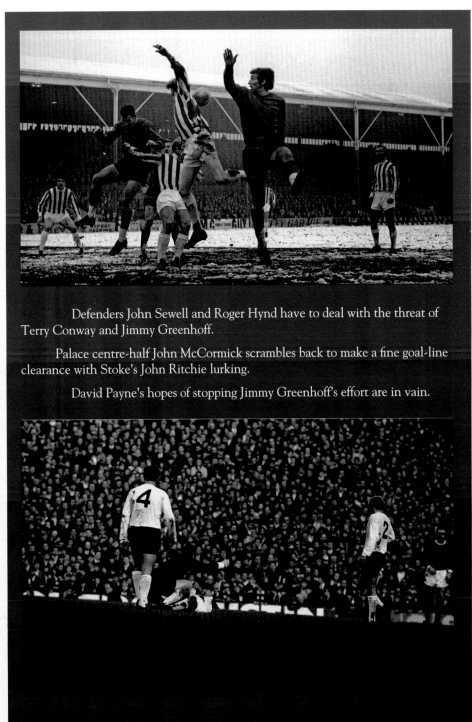

Defenders John Sewell and Roger Hynd have to deal with the threat of Terry Conway and Jimmy Greenhoff.

Palace centre-half John McCormick scrambles back to make a fine goal-line clearance with Stoke's John Ritchie lurking.

David Payne's hopes of stopping Jimmy Greenhoff's effort are in vain.

Of course, games against London rivals always came with a bit of added spice and this festive meeting between Palace and Chelsea, which took place on 27th December 1969, was no different. Sadly for the home side, any Christmas cheer had evaporated by the end of the game with Chelsea winning 5-1. Peter Osgood got four of the Chelsea goals while Gerry Queen scored for the home side, the demolition bringing a dismal end to what, on the whole, had been a positive year.

LEFT: Keeper John Jackson picks a cross off the head of Chelsea's Ian Hutchison with Hynd looking on.

BELOW: The two sides get to grips with each other as the spirit of Christmas wears thin. Chelsea's no. 9 Peter Osgood scored four goals but was lucky not to be sent off when he found himself in the thick of an ugly brawl. As he told newspaper reporters after the game: "I was fortunate not to get in trouble. I lost my head."

PAGE 18 DAILY MIRROR, Monday December 29 1969

'NO PANIC BUYING' IN CRISIS FOR HEAD

CRYSTAL PALACE will not be pushed into panic buying despite growing fears that their promotion-winning team are not good enough to keep them in the First Division.

By NIGEL CLARKE

Suddenly, that goodwill spirit is forgotten

PETER OSGOOD turned on a remarkable four-goal show at Selhurst Park on Saturday as Chelsea swamped Crystal Palace 5—1. He was also lucky to stay on the field when the match exploded into an ugly brawl. As Osgood (No. 9, above) admitted later: "I was fortunate not to get into trouble. I lost my head."

Despite the delight of being in Division One, there was no escaping the fact that Palace were struggling and that defeat by Chelsea was yet another in a miserable run. A 2-1 victory over Wolverhampton Wanderers on 22nd November 1969, in which Trevor Dawkins scored both goals, would be Palace's last triumph until the following March. Four draws and nine defeats followed before the rot was finally stopped on 11th March 1970 with a 1-0 win, thanks to a Gerry Queen goal, over Manchester City at Maine Road. In all, Head's side had managed just three wins in the first half of the season and a battle to remain in the division lay ahead. Nevertheless, the manager was adamant he wouldn't be panicked into splashing some cash to keep his side up, as the *Mirror* reported on 29th December 1969.

One of the draws in that sequence came against Manchester United at Old Trafford on St Valentine's Day, 14th February 1970. John Sewell scored Palace's goal in a 1-1 draw, meaning the club were unbeaten in the League against the Manchester giants that season. Palace ended the season third from bottom, but with only two teams going down, survived for another crack at Division One.

United legend Bobby Charlton fails to connect with a cross while (inset) David Payne is delighted as he watches John Sewell's equalizer go over the line.

We players expected a really tough struggle in our first season in the First Division, but we did not expect it to be quite so desperate and nerve-wracking as it was.

John Sewell

85

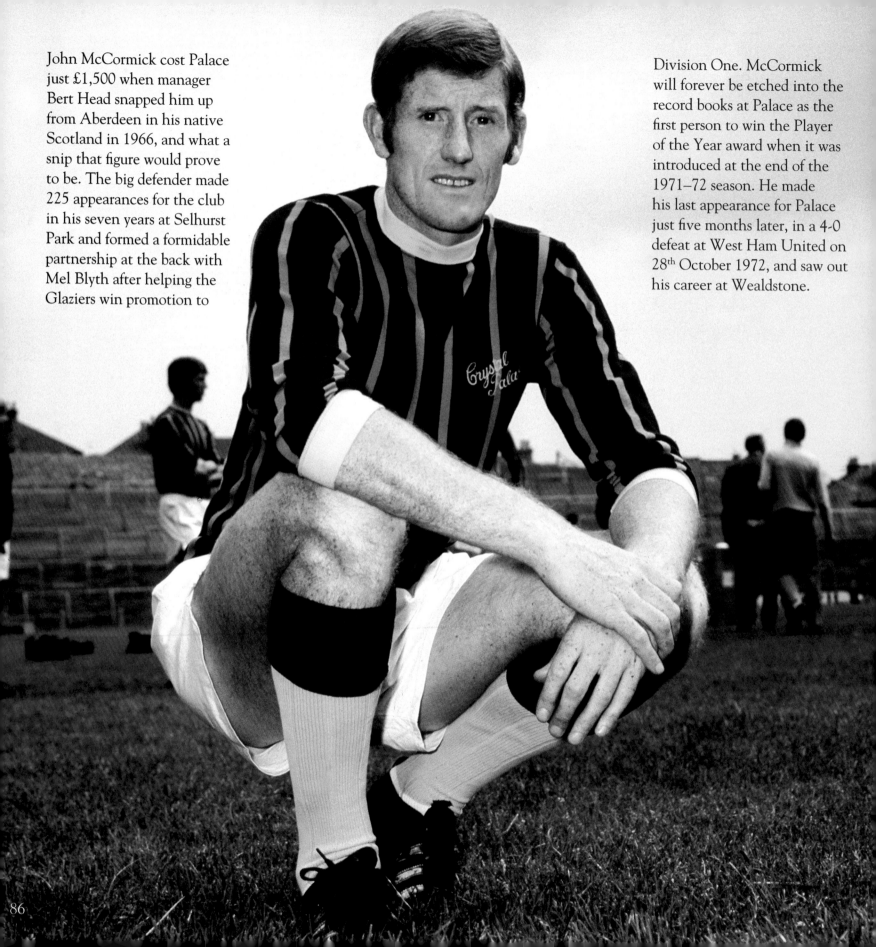

John McCormick cost Palace just £1,500 when manager Bert Head snapped him up from Aberdeen in his native Scotland in 1966, and what a snip that figure would prove to be. The big defender made 225 appearances for the club in his seven years at Selhurst Park and formed a formidable partnership at the back with Mel Blyth after helping the Glaziers win promotion to

Division One. McCormick will forever be etched into the record books at Palace as the first person to win the Player of the Year award when it was introduced at the end of the 1971–72 season. He made his last appearance for Palace just five months later, in a 4-0 defeat at West Ham United on 28th October 1972, and saw out his career at Wealdstone.

The summer of 1970 saw manager Bert Head sell three players – Cliff Jackson, Roger Hoy and Roger Hynd – and bring in three more with top-fight experience. These were left-back Peter Wall from Liverpool for £25,000 and strikers Bobby Tambling and Alan Birchenall in a double deal from London rivals Chelsea. Tambling had spent three months on loan at Selhurst Park at the end of the previous season and the two men would cost a combined £140,000 as they were both snapped up on a permanent basis. Birchenall scored 14 goals for Palace in 48 appearances – he was Palace's leading scorer in the League with 10 – in all competitions that season but was sold to Leicester City a year later for £100,000.

Striker Alan Birchenall applies the powder for a not-exactly-reluctant Steve Kember ahead of an appearance on ITV's *On The Ball* on 10th September 1970.

One man remained constant while Head was chopping and changing his squad, and that was goalkeeper John Jackson. The big man was never afraid to challenge anyone for any ball and this picture was typical of him. It was taken during a 0-0 draw at Stoke City on 29th August 1970, and shows Jackson and Denis Smith doing battle. Even when Jackson was in relaxed mood posing in his goalmouth – this time ahead of a 3-1 victory over Southampton, thanks to two goals from Gerry Queen and one from Alan Birchenall at Selhurst Park on 3rd October the same year – there was something of the Bond villain about him. Jaws, anyone?

Outside-right Jim Scott joined Palace from Newcastle during the 1969–70 campaign and left for Falkirk in his native Scotland after making 50 appearances for the club. He is pictured here during a 2-1 win over Ipswich at Selhurst Park on 5th December 1970. Jim Sewell (from the penalty spot) and Steve Kember got the goals that day.

Steve Kember, Mel Blyth and John Jackson look on as a cross intended for Ray Kennedy of Arsenal skids across goal. The Division One game at Highbury on 14th November 1970 ended in a 1-1 draw, with Alan Birchenall scoring for Palace.

Alan Birchenall, Gerry Queen and Steve Kember talk tactics the old-fashioned way ahead of Palace's 1970–71 FA Cup third-round tie with Chelsea on 2nd January. John McCormick and Birchenall bagged the goals for Palace in a 2-2 draw at Selhurst Park. Chelsea won the replay four days later, 2-0.

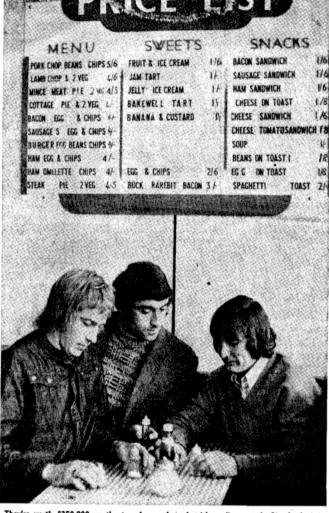

PAGE 14   DAILY MIRROR, Friday, January 1, 1971

Cup special

A WARNING TO ARSENAL: DON'T PLAY IT CLEVER

By

KEN JONES

YEOVIL'S last hopeful excursion into the third round of the FA Cup ended in disillusion six years ago when they ran into a then Second Division club unashamedly playing Fourth Division football.

The club was Bury, their player-manager Bob Stokoe, who was this week appointed to try to rescue Blackpool from the prospect of relegation.

Stokoe starts with a Cup-tie of his own against West Ham, but last night recalled that he once deliberately aimed his best clearances into a Cup crowd at Yeovil.

He says: "I don't expect Arsenal to lose there because First Division clubs have entirely changed their attitude to this sort of match since the days when I first started playing Cup football with Newcastle.

Determined

"Anything could happen then—and usually did. It was all a bit haphazard. Players now have the benefit of what we had to put up with and we impress upon them that no one has a divine right to anything in this game.

"A non-League club playing at home against famous opponents used to have the advantage of knowing that star players might not relish being met with enthusiasm and determination. On little grounds with the crowd breathing down their necks the big teams often ran into trouble.

Put Out

"They would start trying to push the ball around and then find that they were being overrun and put out of the game.

"Look what once hap-pened to Sunderland at Yeovil. That remains Yeovil's most famous victory and it was an example of things that were going on in the game at that time.

"When I went to Yeovil with Bury we were on a hiding to nothing because we were little more than an ordinary Second Division side.

"Arsenal have better players than I had but I am sure their policy will be similar to the one we adopted.

Squeeze

"We went out there to run as hard to fight as hard and to go in as bravely as Yeovil were prepared to do.

"We met them on their own terms and fought for the right to show that we were a different class.

"That's what these games are all about. It's no good trying to look clever. These little teams keep running, keep coming at you and it's no good waiting for them to run out of steam.

"You've got to squeeze the steam out of them. It's not pretty but these matches are all about winning."

Bob-sled

Arsenal with their studied approach to every match will not need reminding that Yeovil could give them a problem tomorrow.

Yeovil's pitch is rapidly taking on the character of a bob-sled run.

Warm sunshine has not penetrated the frost which grips the lower third of their slope and unless there is a thaw it could become a nightmare test of balance and only the bravest will be willing to play there.

Yeovil's team was announced almost casually last night after player-Mike Hughes had elected for the experience of Ken Thompson over the youthful exuberance of teenager Andy McCluskey.

It is the one change from the team which beat Bournemouth in the last round.

If the hard frost continues there will clearly be some concern over the state of the pitch and Swansea referee Bill Gow moves in today to be on hand for an early inspection.

They're worth £350,000 on the transfer market—but it's no dinner at the Ritz for former Chelsea star Alan Birchenall (left) and his Crystal Palace team-mates Gerry Queen (centre) and Steve Kember. Just tactics talk in the local cafe on how to knock Chelsea out of the Cup tomorrow.
Picture: MONTE FRESCO

Jackson Fives

John Jackson takes exception to a challenge from Coventry's Brian Joicey on 20th February 1971. The game ended in a 2-1 defeat for Palace, with Alan Birchenall getting the Eagles' only goal.

The big games and big names kept coming thick and fast for Palace, with Arsenal the visitors to Selhurst Park on 13th March 1971. The Gunners won the game 2-0 to add to the home side's concerns over relegation.

Steve Kember chases down Arsenal's Peter Storey.

Bobby Tambling spent three months on loan at Selhurst Park from Chelsea at the end of the 1969–70 campaign and signed on a permanent contract ahead of the following season. He had set the record as Chelsea's all-time leading scorer during his time at Stamford Bridge and arrived at Palace with bundles of top-flight experience and a proven ability to score. He wasn't as prolific with the Glaziers as he had been at his previous club, but still managed 17 goals in 76 appearances over four years.

Tambling lets rip with a shot in the game against Manchester United at Selhurst Park on 17th April 1971. His goal that day was sandwiched by strikes from Alan Birchenall and Gerry Queen but, sadly for the home fans, United hit five in reply. It had been another difficult campaign in the top tier for Palace but Head, once again, steered them to safety, a fifth-from-bottom finish ensuring they would be a Division One side again for the 1971–72 season.

Crystal Palace's pre-season photocall at Selhurst Park in July 1971. Back row, left to right: John McCormick, Alan Birchenall, John Hardie, John Jackson, Mel Blyth and Gerry Queen. Middle row: Alan Pinkney, Dave Payne, Peter Wall, Steve Kember, Phil Hoadley, Bobby Tambling, Terry Wharton. Front row: Terry Long (trainer), Tony Taylor, Gerry Humphreys, John Loughlan, Jim Scott, Bert Head (manager).

Steve Kember might have been idolized by the Selhurst Park faithful but his relationship with the club didn't always run smoothly. There had been talk of him leaving Palace in 1971 and he had asked for a move, but in the end differences were thrashed out and supporters awoke on the morning of 8th August 1971 to learn that their favourite midfielder had signed a new deal.

PAGE 26   DAILY MIRROR, Thursday, August 12, 1971

NOW KEMBER MAKES PEACE WITH PALACE

By NIGEL CLARKE

STEVE KEMBER will extend his stay as Crystal Palace skipper this morning by signing a new contract at Selhurst Park.

At present he has three years to run on his contract, two of them on option. The new contract is for two years with a two-year option.

The little mid-field man, rated at around £150,000 on the transfer market, also collects a substantial improvement in terms.

The differences that threatened to open a rift between him and the club, have now been healed—and Kember, who at one time put in for a move, is now content to stay at Palace.

He said last night: "You can say that I'm happy for the moment, and will be doing my best to give the club the kind of start we had last season.

"I've talked things over with manager Bert Head, and am satisfied that we made the right decision.

"I can now fully concentrate on my football again. I've my future to look after — I'm getting

married next month — so obviously it was the sensible thing to do."

Says manager Head: "Steve's future is now very much wrapped up in the club."

Goalkeeper John Jackson and forward Tony Taylor will also follow Kember in to sign similar contracts today.

Meanwhile Palace hope to name their new coach in time for the opening match of the season against Newcastle at Selhurst Park on Saturday.

Rebel

Southampton pay rebel Tommy Jenkins, who earlier this week asked for a move, last night signed a new two-year contract with the club.

The £60,000 winger had talks with manager Ted Bates and said: "My new terms are much better, I'm much happier now."

But Chelsea centre half John Dempsey and Millwall's striker sweeper Dennis Burnett are still in dispute with their clubs over new contracts.

Dempsey is to take his case to the independent tribunal as the Football League have turned down his appeal.

"I'm getting in touch with PFA secretary Cliff Lloyd for further guidance. There's no question of me wanting to leave the club, it's just that I feel I'm entitled to a little more money."

Burnett's request for a rise has also been turned down by the Millwall board. "It's getting to the stage now when I'll have to think about asking for a transfer," he told me last night.

Sorting out his problems . . . Crystal Palace skipper Steve Kember at the club's Beckenham training ground yesterday.   Picture: MONTE FRESCO.

Skipper who 'had to tell the truth'

STEVE KEMBER
'Sorry for Forest'

CRYSTAL PALACE skipper Steve Kember brought sanity back to Soccer on Saturday with one of the few honest actions in a season simmering with controversy.

Yesterday, he told me why he had admitted to referee Ron Judson that a goal he had allowed Palace was never in the Nottingham Forest net.

Terry Wharton's fierce drive had struck Forest defender Bob Chapman on the chest and gone for a corner. Judson awarded a goal-kick, but linesman Fred Webb signalled a goal.

Kember said: "When the referee asked me if it was a goal, I had to say no The game is in a bad enough state as it is.

"I couldn't believe it when the referee pointed towards the middle. I am certain that if I had not spoken up, and the goal had stood, Forest would never have kicked off again

"They would have just walked off the field, and who could have blamed them? I felt sorry for them."

Checked

Play was held up for five minutes as Forest protested and the referee checked with his linesman again. The net was inspected for holes, and police asked enraged Forest manager Matt Gillies to leave the pitch.

Kember went on: "The referee said to me that he had to make a fair decision. I had to tell the truth.

"I was very tempted to say it was a goal, and that point could well be vitally important if we struggle around the foot of the table this season.

"As it was, it was probably the only way we could have won the match.

"I'll commit every professional foul in the book, but I could not honestly live with a lie.

"I was the nearest player to the incident, but the referee shouldn't have asked me my opinion. After all, he was in charge of the match."

Forest captain Peter Hindley said: "Steve did well for us.

"All the Palace players were telling him to say it

By NIGEL CLARKE

was a goal. You can't blame them. I would have said so myself if it had happened to us.

"But it was a diabolical decision—Steve just sorted it out for the best."

Forest vice - chairman Tony Wood described it as "a great act of sportsmanship by Kember."

He added: "The referee gave a goal kick and the linesman flagged for a goal, when the right decision should have been a corner

"Then the referee went to inspect the net for holes. There would have had to be one as big as your head for a ball to go through. How could it have been a goal?"

Poor

The incident came after seventy-six minutes, with the score 1—1. And that was how a poor game finished.

Both teams have major problems to solve if they want to climb to a position of safety in the First Division

Palace need a midfield man and another front player. Forest at least one back-four man. It was here that Forest struggled most.

Palace went ahead when Alan Birchenall snapped up a loose ball that twice should have been cleared.

An error by defender Mel Blyth let Forest's Duncan McKenzie in for the equaliser.

Kember was an honest pro in every sense, hard-working and hard-tackling, but he played the game in the right spirit as well, as the *Mirror* reported on 30th August 1971. Despite having signed new terms at Palace just three weeks earlier, however, things weren't as rosy as perhaps they were being portrayed . . .

Kember is captured during a pre-season training session on 13th August 1971, having just been appointed Palace captain.

The revolving door at Selhurst Park was still spinning into September 1971 as Bert Head continued to reshape his squad and, naturally, the *Mirror* reported on all of the comings and goings. Steve Kember left the club for Chelsea only a month after signing his new deal and his departure on the back of Alan Birchenall's switch to Leicester was big news. Head was honest enough to admit that he felt the big changes were necessary and he brought in several new players. Central defender Bobby Bell and midfielders Bobby Kellard and John Craven were signed, while utility man Sam Goodwin's transfer was about to be sealed.

WELLER FOR LEICESTER..
That's £100,000 Bloomfield target

LEICESTER will be first in the queue when Chelsea begin to reduce a first-team squad that now numbers eighteen players, writes Nigel Clarke.

And I understand they are ready to pay £100,000 for Keith Weller who finished last season as leading scorer at Stamford Bridge.

Immediately after signing Alan Birchenall from Crystal Palace in a £100,000 deal on Tuesday, Leicester chief Jimmy Bloomfield promised another six-figure signing.

Weller, who has played only two first team games this season, because of illness and injury, is his target. Meanwhile Weller, who can operate wide on the wing or inside, played in the reserves on Wednesday and aggravated an old foot injury.

It may keep him out of action for another week, and he said last night: "I'm hoping it is not too serious, but it may take some time to get better."

Weller was struck down with a mystery virus after Chelsea's close season tour of Sweden. He was in hospital a week, and only recently returned to full training.

Chelsea boss Dave Sexton now has such a strong squad that he has four men competing for the three midfield positions, and five contesting the three forward places.

And Steve Kember, £170,000 signing from Crystal Palace on Wednesday, may well have to wait for his first team debut.

Content

Sexton may keep the side who drew with Derby 1—1 last week for the match against League leaders Sheffield United. Kember could then be fitted in after the second leg of the European Cup Winners Cup against Jeunesse Hautcharage of Luxembourg next Wednesday.

Sam Kember: "I've been told that I may not be in at first, and I understand the reasons. I'm content to wait for my chance."

JUMPING to it—still, it's hard to keep your feet on the ground if your name's Steve Kember and you've just cost £170,000.
Picture: MONTE FRESCO

RIOCH NEXT FOR PALACE
That's Head's new £100,000 target

By NIGEL CLARKE

CRYSTAL PALACE'S next target in a week of transfer fever seems certain to be Bruce Rioch, Aston Villa's £100,000 utility player.

Palace, who so far have bought three players—and are banking on another—with the £270,000 received from selling off Alan Birchenall and Steve Kember, have been interested in Rioch for some time.

Chief coach Dave Ewing watched him in action against Mansfield on Wednesday night, and Palace, who still have more than £100,000 left to spend, are in a position to push a deal through.

I understand they have failed to tempt Spurs to part with Jimmy Pearce and Tony Want, but are keeping a close watch on Carlisle striker Bob Hatton.

Switch?

So if the Rioch bid falls through, Palace may switch their interests to Hatton.

Meanwhile, they paid out £55,000 yesterday for Blackburn defender Bobby Bell, and agreed terms at around £30,000 with Airdrie for midfield man Sammy Goodwin.

Bell's transfer is extraordinary. He only moved from Ipswich three weeks ago in a part exchange deal with Irish international Allan Hunter.

Now he lines up with Wednesday signings Bobby Kellard, £50,000 from Leicester, and John Craven, £37,500 from Blackpool, against Everton at Selhurst Park on Saturday.

Palace chairman Arthur Wait said: "What we needed was a really good shake-up. We had to turn the side inside out. It was the only way to raise enough cash to buy new players.

"This course of action was decided at a board meeting on Saturday.

"Certain decisions were taken that we knew wouldn't be popular, but it was equally certain that something had to be done.

"We were determined that there would be some movement in the transfer market this week.

"Of course it is a wrench having to sell your best players, especially Kember. He wasn't just the skipper of the side, he grew up with us.

Action

"But you must be realistic. The set-up was not right, and action was needed. We have taken only three points from nine games and are bottom of the First Division.

THE TRANSFER ROUNDABOUT	
BERT HEAD, manager of bottom of the table Crystal Palace, has spent a busy three days in the transfer market in an effort to revitalise his struggling team. He has:	**BOUGHT**
SOLD	£55,000 BOBBY BELL from Blackburn
£170,000 STEVE KEMBER to Chelsea	£50,000 BOBBY KELLARD from Leicester
£100,000 ALAN BIRCHENALL to Leicester	£37,500 JOHN CRAVEN from Blackpool
	PENDING
	£30,000 SAM GOODWIN from Airdrie

Obviously that was not satisfactory."

Manager Bert Head said: "I have been turned down recently in my efforts to get new players because I haven't had the money to buy them. This is the only way I can get the money I need.

"I am aiming at overall strength, though. I realise I cannot match Kember's class. But I do feel we can get a better all-round blend.

"We've not finished improving the team yet . . . I hope to sign one more player."

Palace may not have finished unloading yet.

Backing

"Palace must be applauded for realising the general situation and doing something about it. We must back them over this.

Last word from Head: "I don't really want to comment on it, but supporters said we were wrong to sell Alan Stephenson yet with the money we received for him, we were able to buy other players that brought the club promotion.

"Only time will tell if we have been right or wrong."

The FRANK O'FARRELL Column

Both Millwall and Preston have made inquiries about centre forward Gerry Queen, and Head may well listen if he gets the right offer.

But Palace's transfer market activity could cost the club support. Many fans, still stunned at the week's events, have threatened to boycott Selhurst Park.

Stan Whitby, secretary of the supporters club, said: "This is a positive effort to improve things at the club and we must wait and see how it works out."

NOW CHEER UP, PALACE

By HARRY MILLER

CRYSTAL PALACE fans were urged last night to support the club's moves to rebuild their team in a battle for First Division survival.

Before manager Bert Head went home for "a good sleep" at the end of a week of non-stop transfer activity, he called on the Selhurst Park crowd to cheer Palace to victory against Everton today.

Bobby Kellard, Bobby Bell and John Craven—for whom Palace paid £140,0000—all play this afternoon. And this was Head's answer to the threat that Palace supporters will openly criticise the shock £270,000 exit of Steve Kember and Alan Birchenall!

"Something had to be done. Our supporters will have their chance to judge whether it is the right thing.

Support

"We think it is. But the team we have re-constructed needs their support. I hope they give it against Everton, and in the games to come.

"After all, it probably won't all come right overnight.

"It would have been different if we were top of the League. We're not. We're at the bottom with three points, and we are going nowhere.

"Things just haven't gone right this season. It all boiled to the surface in the second half at Tot-tenham last Saturday. We were terrible.

"That was crisis point."

Head in crisis plea to fans

"What has happened this week isn't just my doing. We had a board meeting on Sunday when the decisions were taken.

"Kember and Birchenall were sold after we were sure of their replacements at the prices we wanted.

"These players will do well for us. Kellard, for instance, has a heck of a lot to offer.

"He was a great favourite with the crowd when he was previously a Palace player. His heart is in this club. And he's a great professional.

"So are Bell and Craven. And all three have been club captains."

Head sat in his office while TV and Press cameramen took pictures of his new players out on the pitch.

"The spirit out there, among the players, is great," he said. "We're buzzing again. You can feel it in the air."

Sammy Goodwin, Airdrie midfield star, will become Palace's fourth new player when he signs on Tuesday for a £30,000 fee.

Head looks certain to complete his map hand by moving firmly for an additional striker.

Last night the choice rested between Coventry's John O'Rourke—also wanted by Queen's Park Rangers—and Carlisle's Bob Hatton.

LEFT: Willie Wallace arrived at Selhurst Park in a joint £55,000 deal with John Hughes from Celtic and is pictured here on his home debut on 30th October 1971 battling with West Ham United's Bryan 'Pop' Robson. It wasn't the best of starts for Wallace, with the Hammers winning 3-0. He spent less than a year at the club, making 42 appearances and scoring six goals in all competitions, before returning north of the border to join Dumbarton.

LEFT: John Craven joined the club from Blackpool and spent two seasons at Selhurst before moving to Coventry City.

RIGHT: Bobby Kellard had two spells at Palace, the first from 1963 to 1966 and the second from 1971 to 1973, and was brought back to replace Steve Kember. It was a big job, but he did it so well that he was eventually rewarded with the captaincy. He is pictured here in July 1972.

Bobby Bell puts in the sort of challenge on Tottenham's Mike England on 27th January 1973, a 0-0 draw at Selhurst Park, that would no doubt earn a straight red card today.

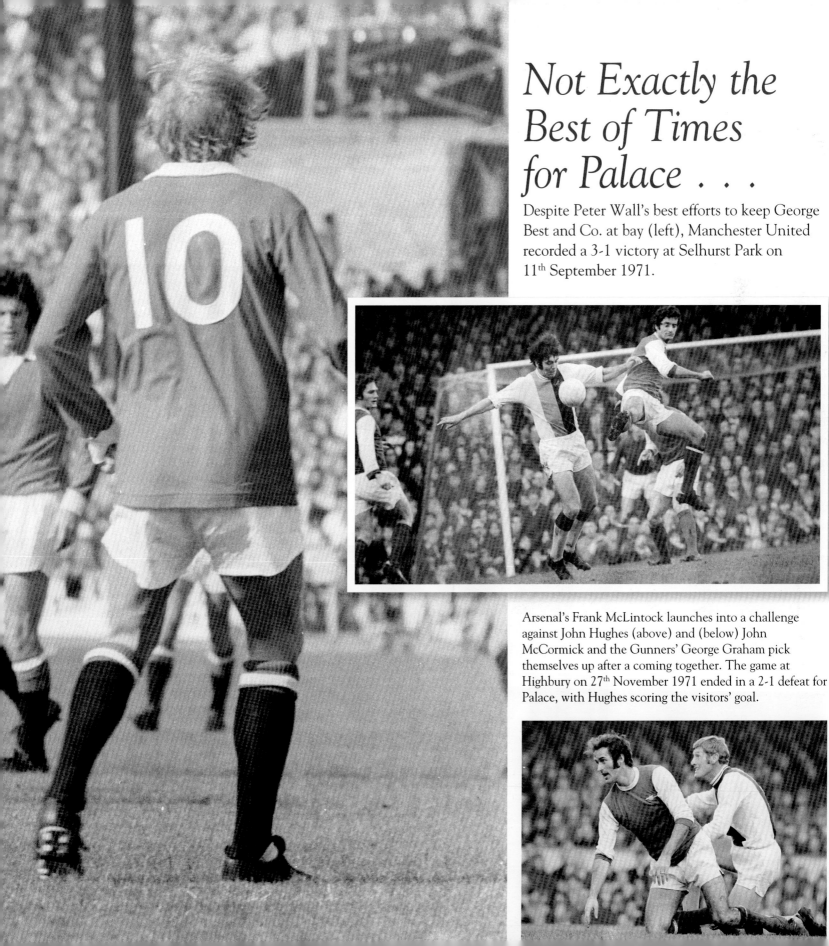

Not Exactly the Best of Times for Palace . . .

Despite Peter Wall's best efforts to keep George Best and Co. at bay (left), Manchester United recorded a 3-1 victory at Selhurst Park on 11th September 1971.

Arsenal's Frank McLintock launches into a challenge against John Hughes (above) and (below) John McCormick and the Gunners' George Graham pick themselves up after a coming together. The game at Highbury on 27th November 1971 ended in a 2-1 defeat for Palace, with Hughes scoring the visitors' goal.

103

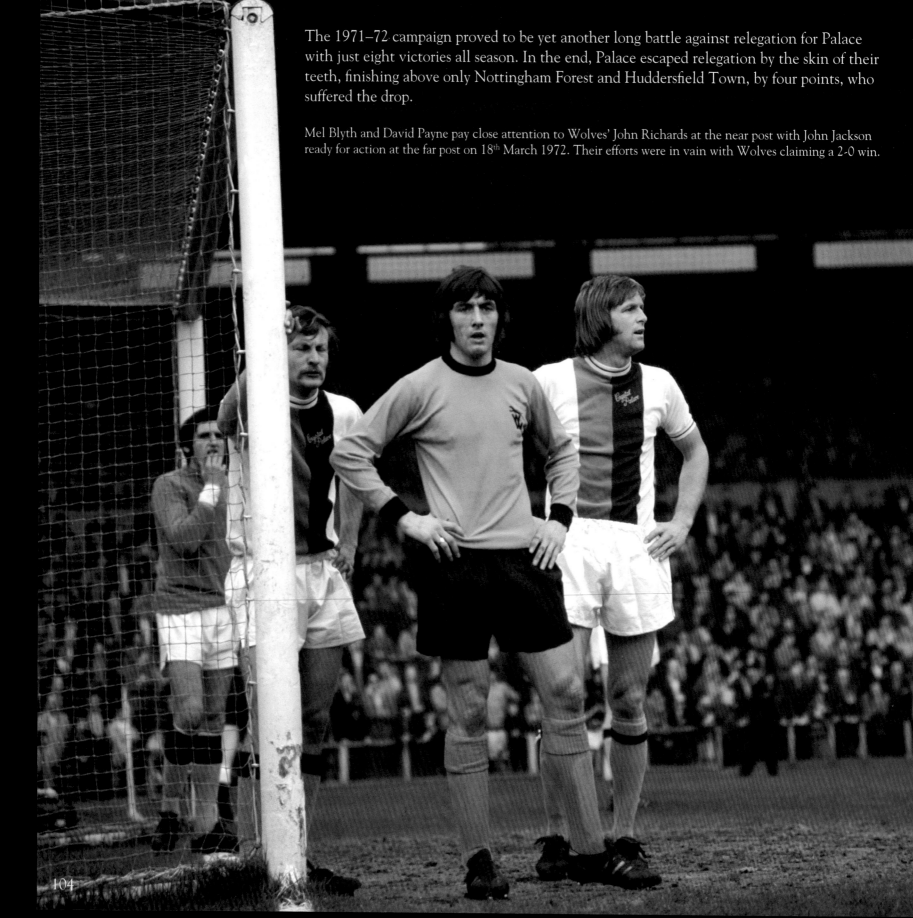

The 1971–72 campaign proved to be yet another long battle against relegation for Palace with just eight victories all season. In the end, Palace escaped relegation by the skin of their teeth, finishing above only Nottingham Forest and Huddersfield Town, by four points, who suffered the drop.

Mel Blyth and David Payne pay close attention to Wolves' John Richards at the near post with John Jackson ready for action at the far post on 18th March 1972. Their efforts were in vain with Wolves claiming a 2-0 win.

—LEGENDS—

Don Rogers

Don Rogers made the perfect start to life as a Palace player when he scored the only goal of the game on his debut against Everton at Selhurst on 4th November 1972. He had been prolific at Swindon Town and would go on to score a further 12 goals in the League for Palace in the 1972–73 campaign. Sadly, his efforts were not enough to keep the club up, but they were appreciated by the fans nonetheless and they took him to their hearts. Rogers was again the top scorer in Division Two the following season, this time with 15 goals, but once again his goals were not enough to keep the Glaziers in their division and he left shortly after the 1973–74 season began with Palace languishing in Division Three.

RIGHT: Rogers poses at the club's pre-season photocall in August 1972.

BELOW: As he told the *Mirror* on 4th November 1972, the step up to the top flight held no worries for Rogers and, as he proved, there had been no need for it to, either.

FOOTBALL —STATS—

Don Rogers

Name: Don Rogers

Born: 25th October 1945 (Paulton)

Playing career: Swindon Town, Crystal Palace, Queens Park Rangers, Swindon Town

Position: Left-winger

Palace appearances: 78 (1972–75)

Palace goals: 30

DAILY MIRROR, Saturday, November 4, 1972. PAGE 31

DAY OF THE DON!

Not a worry as he moves into big-time

DON ROGERS has waited a long time for the chance to play in the First Division—and he intends to make the most of it today.

He steps out for his new club, Crystal Palace, against Everton at Selhurst Park—full of confidence in his own ability.

By JACK STEGGLES

Worried? Of course I'm not—I'm looking forward to it," the former Swindon winger told me last night.

"Everton are a tremendous side who always play attractive football, and I can't tell you how much I've waited for this day.

"I've heard that Palace are in need of a player to take responsibility—someone to hold the ball and take people on.

"I'll do that with pleasure. That's the way I've always played, and I see no reason to change now.

Tough

"I don't think I'm cocky. It's simply that I have been in the game too long to be over-awed.

"I know it will be tough. The pace in the First Division is so much faster—I've backed that pass to training.

"Despite the run of poor results, there is a good spirit among the

lads and we are all confident of our ability to climb out of trouble.

"I shall certainly be doing all I can to improve the position, to repay manager Bert Head for signing me.

"I thought the chance of First Division football had gone, but Bert had enough confidence to come in for me.

As I revealed yesterday, Palace have called up "forgotten" Bobby Bell in place of John McCormick at centre-half, and big scot John Hughes gets a front-line spot.

Goalkeeper John Jackson and full-back Paddy Mulligan line return after injury.

Injuries rule out Paul Hinshelwood and Bobby Tambling. McCormick and enough confidence to Paul Hammond and Alan Pinkney are dropped.

Ready to mow down Everton! £150,000 signing, with skipper Paddy Mulligan. Don Rogers, Crystal Palace's new Picture: ERIC PIPER

New boys Paddy Mulligan, Iain Philip, Charlie Cooke and Don Rogers line up ahead of the game against Everton on 4th November 1972 in which Rogers, making his debut, would score the only goal of the game. It was Palace's first win in nine matches – a dismal run which included eight defeats.

'MR PALACE' WALKS OUT

A wind of change had blown through Selhurst Park a fortnight prior to that victory over Everton and, while the win brought a brief respite on the field, it could not paper over the cracks which had started to appear off it. Long-serving chairman Arthur Wait had become life-president after stepping aside for Raymond Bloye but, on 6th November 1972, he declared his intention to walk out on the club for good because of politics behind the scenes. Wait's decision was published in the *Mirror* the day after and was the second time the club had made headlines in two days.

Bloye's Brigade

Wait: I don't want any more of the niggling

ARTHUR WAIT walked out last night —for good—on the club that was his life.

Wait, who became Crystal Palace's life-president when he resigned as chairman two weeks ago, said: "I'm finished. There's power politics here now."

It was a decision that stunned new chairman Ray Bloye, who told me: "I'm very hurt, and absolutely astounded. I knew nothing about it.

"I was more than happy to work under Mr Wait — it was he who brought me into football.

"But until I study the situation I don't want to make any further comment."

By NIGEL CLARKE

ARTHUR WAIT
"complete break."

Reign

Wait, 62-year-old builder, reigned as "Mr. Palace" for twenty-two years, in which the club rose from the Fourth Division to the First.

But last night he said: "I don't want any more of the backbiting and niggling — doing things when I'm not there.

"I'm unhappy with the treatment I've received over the last two weeks, and am making a complete break from Palace.

"Since resigning as chairman I have not been invited to a board meeting—and I believe there have been a few.

"Our club hospitality has always been second to none. Now there seems to be a cold wind of change.

"I was given a yellow card on Saturday to be shown to gain admittance to the boardroom. I told them what to do with it.

"No one was going to stop me going in.

"A supporter also requested a record to be played for me—and they refused.

"There was a row because I went to Swindon with manager Bert Head to sign Don Rogers.

"Well, that's the last player I help bring to the club. I have asked to be relieved of all financial commitments."

GREGG IN CHARGE

Harry Gregg, former Manchester United and Ireland goalkeeper, was last night named Swansea's new manager. Gregg, 37, who recently resigned as boss of Shrewsbury, replaces Roy Bentley.

PALACE STRAIN

He plans talks with boss to discuss his future after shock sending-off

By NIGEL CLARKE
Crystal Palace 1, Everton 0

Mel Blyth is sent off. *Picture: MIKE LLOYD*

Twenty-four hours earlier, the *Mirror* had dropped with Mel Blyth citing tensions on the field for his dismissal against Everton and those problems would signal the beginning of the end for Palace's stay in the top flight.

108

Raymond Bloye was chairman of Crystal Palace from 1972 to 1981 and his first major task at the helm was to identify a new manager when Bert Head resigned on 30th March 1973 with the club fighting for survival in Division One. Bloye turned to the flamboyant Malcolm Allison and the pair are pictured here just a couple of days later on 1st April with England manager Sir Alf Ramsey.

With Palace back in Division Two and under new leadership both on and off the field, the time felt right for historical changes at the club, too. A new badge was introduced ahead of the 1973–74 season and the colours of claret and sky blue became the red-and-blue stripes which are still worn today. Palace's nickname was switched as well, from the Glaziers to the Eagles.

Much attention was paid to the club's new crest at the pre-season photocall ahead of the 1973–74 campaign and star man Don Rogers and new manager Malcolm Allison made a point of drawing attention to it as they posed in August 1973.

111

—LEGENDS—

Jim Cannon

It wasn't all doom and gloom at Palace in the early Seventies, just mostly, but the emergence of Jim Cannon through the ranks would at least provide the fans with one constant against all the turmoil which seemed to be taking place behind the scenes. Cannon was born in Scotland, but was picked up by manager Bert Head as a 16-year-old and brought to London as a junior. He made his first-team debut on 31st March 1973 against Chelsea, in a 2-0 victory in which Iain Philip scored the first goal and Cannon scored the second. That start won the fans over immediately and the relationship would be cemented over the next 16 years, for 10 of which Cannon was captain of the club.

RIGHT: Cannon jumps with former Palace favourite Dave Swindlehurst, by now of Derby County, on 24th October 1981, during a 1-0 defeat at Selhurst Park.

FOOTBALL —STATS—

Jim Cannon

Name: Jim Cannon

Born: 2nd October 1953 (Glasgow)

Playing career: Crystal Palace, Bristol Rovers

Position: Defender

Palace appearances: 659 (1972–88)

Palace goals: 35

Cannon larks about on 10th October 1978 at Palace's training ground.

> *He scored goals, he'd dribble past three or four players and for a centre-half you'd never heard of it. Jim should have gone bigger, he had the ability.*
>
> Kenny Sansom

> *You get to a certain stage where you think, 'I wouldn't mind being skipper'. I think everybody knows their own temperament and I felt it was a job I would eventually do.*
>
> Jim Cannon

Malcolm Allison was one of football's most colourful characters of the Seventies . . . and that was saying something. Features like this one, which appeared in the *Mirror* on 8th May 1973, were a regular occurrence, and at times it could seem as if as much newsprint at the front end of a newspaper was given to Big Mal as in the sports pages at the back. There was no doubting Allison loved the champagne lifestyle, but he at least brought some glitz and glamour to Selhurst Park at a time when there was little else to celebrate.

DAILY MIRROR, Tuesday, May 8, 1973   PAGE 21

BOB STOKOE.

DON REVIE.

After Bob Stokoe's hat and Don Revie's coat, the Mirror moves in to smarten up that dreary touchline image..

Beau Mal!

MALCOLM ALLISON may be a Second Division manager but he's a top league dresser. Big Mal, 45, of Crystal Palace, believes there's nothing in the rules that says Soccer bosses should be slouches when it comes to clothes off the pitch.

It's a point Messrs. Stokoe (favourite garment a pork pie hat) and Revie (figure-hugging sheepskin) might take up.

Malcolm, who is 6ft. 1½in. in his deodorised socks, has the kind of frame that gives tailors (and women) problems. It's not easy to find ready-to-wear gear when you have a 44½in. chest and bulging biceps enlarged by daily weight-lifting.

Suits

A lot of those fashion problems have been sorted out since he came into the £13,000 a year bracket! Because now Malcolm—an ambitious Virgoan — can afford thirteen tailor-made suits in his wardrobe, two dozen shirts, eight pairs of shoes, and twenty ties.

Being so beautiful can have its problems, of course. Women tend to give him a tough time—if you call fobbing them off hard work.

"Yes, we do get women after us in this game," he says, narrowing his steely-brown eyes. "But I'm old-fashioned. I like to do the chasing—at least, I used to before I married," he adds hastily.

A fact that his wife, Beth, appreciates.

Drink

He has been seen around town lately with ex-Bunny girl Serena Williams, 25, whom he has known for eight years.

"I wouldn't be human if I didn't like pretty ladies," he says firmly. "Once you stop looking, you're dead. But my wife, Beth, knows how I feel about her."

And if Big Mal—favourite drink Dom Perignon Champagne — ever falls foul of the referee he can always take up a new career—as a model.

MAL ABOUT TOWN
DANDY two-tone velvet bow tie, £2.50, and pleated pure silk shirt, £21—both from Turnbull & Asser. The evening cape and cane are from Moss Bros. hire department.

DRESSED TO KILL?
GODFATHER Allison in pinstripe three-piece suit, £29.95, from Lord John. Shirt, £8.50, and boldly checked tie £6.60, from Turnbull & Asser. Smoky velour hat, £15.75, from Blades.

BARE-CHESTED BEEFCAKE
BEEFCAKE patchwork chamois leather shirt from the Battle of Little Big Horn, worn open to show mock Aztec medallion nestling on genuine hairy chest. Plain blue jeans get a tooled belt, £36, from Blades.

PICTURES: TERRY O'NEILL

Still, there was the serious business of football for Allison to attend to, as well as the social engagements, and managing a club, particularly Palace at the time, required a strong character. As the *Mirror* reported on 22nd September 1973, Allison had to get tough with his players and tell them to shape-up or ship out after they made an awful start to the Division Two campaign. His words didn't exactly have the required effect, however, and it was 10th November before they finally won their first League game of the season with a 1-0 victory over Bristol City thanks to an Alan Whittle goal. Things didn't get much better then, though, and with Palace still struggling on 15th January 1974 it was kicking off left, right and centre at the club, as the *Mirror* reported.

Tinker Taylor

By the time the final game of the season came around on 30th April 1974, Palace were still fighting desperately to avoid relegation, having won just 11 games of the 41 they had played. Swindon Town and Preston North End were already doomed by the last day, but several other clubs, including Palace's hosts Cardiff City, were themselves locked in the battle to beat the drop as well. As this picture shows, Peter Taylor did his best to calm the nerves the day before that fixture and amused his team-mates with his impression of Tommy Cooper, but the smiles were wiped from everybody's faces after the 1-1 draw, in which Stewart Jump scored, which saw the Eagles relegated, as the *Mirror*, on 1st May 1974, then reported.

Mirror Sport

Wednesday, May 1, 1974
Telephone: (STD code 01)—353 0246

NIGHT OF SHOCKS FOR LONDON FANS

Allison's men go sliding —now will he go on as Selhurst Park chief?

PALACE DOWN

By Nigel Clarke

Cardiff 1
C Palace 1

A DREAM was destroyed at Ninian Park last night when Crystal Palace slipped off the precipice they had been treading all season to plunge into the Third Division.

Palace needed to win to save themselves and send Cardiff down. But Welsh Under-23 international Tony Villars doomed Malcolm Allison's team with a magnificent equaliser after Stewart Jump had put Palace in front.

Question

For Allison and the club he has tried to rebuild it means relegation for the second successive season.

And it poses the inevitable question. Will Allison stay at Selhurst Park or be branded a failure or will he move on to begin again?

He told me: " I had no doubts before the game that we would win. I had not felt like that since I was at Manchester City. It is not the worst night of my life but it comes pretty close.

" The last ten minutes of the game for me were terrible. But I feel worse for the lads. They played well and now they're slipping stunned in the dressing room tremendously upset."

Allison had set the scene at the start by walking on to the pitch to urge the Palace fans for support.

And for ten glorious minutes Allison held the lead. They won a cor-

Palace star Peter Taylor walks dejectedly off the Ninian Park pitch

ner out on the right in the twenty-ninth minute.

Peter Taylor curled it in, the ball was lost in a mass of players and Jump scored.

But Cardiff equalised in the thirty-ninth minute. Villars intercepted a pass from Taylor, beat three men in a brilliant run, took a return ball from Gil Reece and shot past Paul Hammond.

Taylor hit a post with a snap shot in the dying seconds of the first half.

And after the interval Cardiff, who sent on substitute Derek Showers for the injured Willie Carlin, felt the full power

of Palace. But Cardiff survived.

● Bert Head, the manager whom Allison replaced at Selhurst Park, last night saw his new side, Southern League Bath City, win promotion to the Premier Division with a 1—0 win at Andover.

HOW THEY FINISHED

BOTTOM OF THE TABLE

	P	W	D	L	F	A	Pts
Cardiff	42	10	16	16	49	62	36
Oxford U.	42	10	16	16	35	46	36
Sheff. Wed.	42	12	11	19	51	63	35
C. Palace	42	11	12	19	43	56	34
Preston	42	9	14	19	40	62	31
Swindon	42	7	11	24	36	72	25

PARAS GUARD KEN

KEN BUCHANAN will be accompanied by six men even tougher and cockier and more capable than he is of handling themselves in a fracas, when he steps into the ring here tonight to challenge the local favourite Antonio Puddu, for the European lightweight title.

His escort will be six specially selected British soldiers from the 16th Parachute Brigade, temporarily stationed on this Italian island for NATO manoeuvres.

" I really don't think Mr. Buchanan could come to very much

From FRANK McGHEE in Cagliari, Sardinia

harm with our chaps around him " was the drawled delightfully understated comment of the young officer who organised the guard at the request of Buchanan's trainer, Freddie Hill.

" If there should be any trouble, just yell out 'Airborne' and there will be reinforcements on the scene right away."

At one stage yesterday Buchanan threatening to

walk out and catch the next plane home, because he still hadn't been paid his purse money in advance.

He also threatened to whack promoter Salvatore Cubeni—and I had to persuade him that this would place him entirely in the wrong.

The knowledge that his cheque has been lodged in a local bank did not really soften his attitude —especially as the banks are closed today, a public holiday.

My forecast? Another win for Buchanan, who has been beaten by only two men in his fifty-five fights.

ALAN BALL

By GRAHAM BAKER

Arsenal 1, QPR 1

BREAKS HIS LEG

ALAN BALL'S international future was thrown into jeopardy when he broke his left leg last night — just seventy-five minutes from the end of the League season at Highbury.

Ball suffered a spiral fracture of the fibula in a tackle on Terry Venables for which Rangers were awarded a free kick.

He lay on the ground in agony, but referee Harry New appeared to wave away Arsenal's trainer.

So Ball was left to hobble off—to be replaced four minutes later.

Sitting

After his leg had been put in plaster, Ball left the ground on crutches.

He will be in plaster for at least three weeks —and will miss seven internationals.

" That's me out of the England tour," he said. " There is no way I can make it in a month. It's a choker.

" It was nobody's fault. I tried to nick the ball off Venables and ended up sitting on my ankle. That's what did it.

" I heard a crack and I knew it had to be bad."

Last month Ball was recalled to England's squad for the home international championship although he had played only 15 minutes of international Soccer since he was sent off against Poland ten months ago.

Missing

Besides the home internationals, he will miss the clash with Argentina and tour matches against East Germany, Bulgaria and Yugoslavia.

Ball's injury took all the gloss from a match that had started with a typical goal by Stan Bowles.

From just outside Arsenal's penalty area, Bowles beat a free-kick over a wall of defenders and in off a post to put Rangers ahead in the fourth minute.

Arsenal nearly equal-

ised a minute before the interval, when a Charlie George free-kick hit the bar.

Arsenal appealed for a penalty, claiming that Tony Hazell had handled. Substitute Brady saved Arsenal a point when he met Armstrong's corner and scored with a low drive in the 85th minute.

Bowles and Mick Leach of Rangers and

Arsenal's Eddie Kelly were booked for fouls, and Arsenal's Pat Rice for dissent.

Goalkeeper Bob Wilson, making his final appearance for Arsenal, received an autographed silver tray from the players and a silver cannon from the directors.

After eleven years with the club, he is going into television.

Printed and Published by THE DAILY MIRROR NEWSPAPERS, Ltd. (01-353 0246) at, and for IPC Newspapers Ltd., Holborn Circus, London, EC1P 1DQ. Registered at the Post Office as a newspaper. © The Daily Mirror Newspapers, Ltd., 1974.

On 18th September 1974, an away trip to Hereford in Division Three might not have seemed particularly significant but it would mark the beginning of Terry Venables' relationship with the club. Venables made his debut in that 2-0 defeat and only remained on the playing staff for the remainder of that season, but he moved up to become a coach on Malcolm Allison's staff and went on to manage the club following Allison's departure in the summer of 1976.

Venables in action against southwest Londoners Tooting & Mitcham in the FA Cup on 27th November 1974. Paul Hinshelwood and Alan Whittle got the goals for Palace in a 2-1 win, but they lost 2-1 in the next round to Plymouth, with Dave Swindlehurst scoring the consolation goal.

There wasn't a great deal to sing and shout about at Selhurst Park in 1975 but sing – or shout, some would say – the Palace players did. They recorded two songs – 'Power to the Palace' and 'Flying High' – and were only too happy to pose for photos to publicize their efforts with coach Terry Venables taking lead vocals.

Plotting a St Valentine's Day Massacre

Palace might have been languishing in the third tier of English football during the 1975–76 campaign, but it was still a memorable season thanks largely to the exploits of Malcolm Allison's side in the FA Cup. Walton & Hersham were the Eagles' victims in the first round with a 1-0 win thanks to a goal from David Kemp, and Millwall were dumped out of the competition in the second round with a 2-1 win at the second attempt. Dave Swindlehurst scored in the 1-1 draw at The Den, and Kemp and Peter Taylor then got the goals in the replay. Scarborough were the next team to be deposed by Palace, with Taylor and Ian Evans on target in a 2-1 victory on the North Sea coast, before the fourth-round draw pitted Palace against the mighty Leeds United. Fearless, Palace returned to Yorkshire and took a famous scalp 1-0 courtesy of a Swindlehurst goal which set up an even bigger clash for the side from the Big Smoke against local rivals Chelsea.

The FA Cup antics of Allison and his men captured the attention of the nation and the *Mirror* brought the Palace boss and his squad together and decked them out in gangster threads, resplendent with Allison's trademark fedora hats, as they prepared for a repeat of their giant-killing act against Leeds, this time against Chelsea. This picture and the article which accompanied it ran on 6th February 1976, and was another example of Allison's ability to transcend sport and gatecrash the paper's news and feature pages.

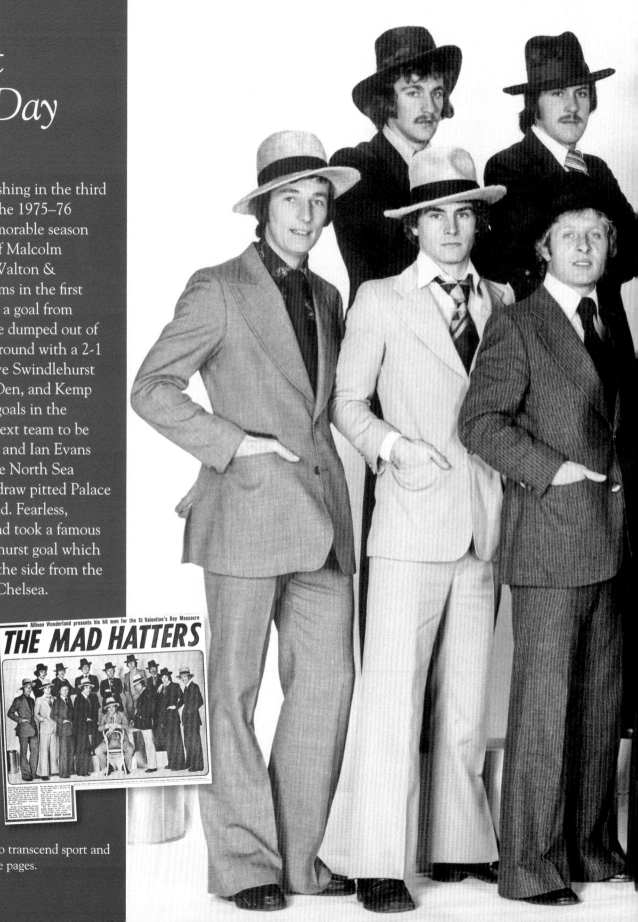

Allison Wonderland presents his hit men for the St Valentine's Day Massacre

THE MAD HATTERS

Beating the Blues

Not even the best efforts of Ron 'Chopper' Harris could stop Peter Taylor and his Palace pals on 14th February 1976 as the Third Division Eagles beat the Division One Blues 3-2. Nobody really believed Palace could follow up their victory over Leeds by claiming another top-flight scalp, but two goals from Taylor and one from Nick Chatterton did the business for Allison's side to set up a sixth-round clash with another Division One outfit, Sunderland, the following month.

Two-goal Taylor skips past 'Chopper' Harris during the 3-2 victory over Chelsea at Selhurst Park.

Palace were on a roll in the FA Cup and, after beating Leeds and Chelsea, there was nothing to fear about a trip to Roker Park to take on Sunderland. Chelsea boss Eddie McCreadie knew that the famous Roker Roar wouldn't faze Allison's side and told the *Mirror* just that on 4th March. Allison and Venables, neither of whom would ever be accused of being the shy and retiring type, and who are pictured here travelling to the Sunderland game by train, were equally effusive about their hopes two days later . . . and with good reason. Palace went on to win the match 1-0, thanks to an Alan Whittle goal, to set up a clash with Southampton in the semi-finals.

Big Mal always put a lot of emphasis on team spirit and his own *joie de vivre* reflected in his men. On 31st March 1976, he and chairman Raymond Bloye took the lads out to a champagne bar in London in the hope that a few glasses of bubbly would bring them even closer together ahead of one of the biggest dates and games in the club's history: 3rd April 1976 and the FA Cup semi-final against Southampton. The match was to be played at the neutral venue of Chelsea's Stamford Bridge.

There was so much anticipation around the clash and Malcolm Allison, as you might expect, wasn't exactly hiding his confidence in the build-up, as the *Mirror* reported on the morning of the game. He was adamant Southampton would be battered by his Third Division minnows and Palace certainly showed plenty of fight, as the main picture shows. Sadly, though, the dream that the Eagles would become the first side from Division Three to reach an FA Cup final did not become a reality and a 2-0 victory ended an incredible run. Still, Palace had every right to be proud of their achievements in the famous old competition that season.

BELOW: Hypnotist Romark – real name Ronald Markham, a former TV and stage illusionist – claimed to have put a curse on Malcolm Allison's side ahead of their FA Cup semi-final as payback for the Palace boss failing to keep an appointment at his Harley Street office. It was utter poppycock, of course, but Romark seemed to get great enjoyment out of watching the Saints' victory on the box all the same.

Malcolm Allison's reign was nothing if not enjoyable for the fans but ultimately he took them from Division One to Division Three and failed to get them back up again. Allison resigned following that FA Cup run, at the end of the 1975–76 season, but despite his lack of success or silverware he had cemented his place in the history of the club. He was a real character, not just for Palace, but the whole of the British game.

"Malcolm Allison put Palace on the map. No other man could single-handedly take a club from the First Division to the Third Division and still become an instant hero."

Jim Cannon

When Allison departed, chairman Ray Bloye promoted coach Terry Venables to the manager's post and, where his predecessor failed, Venables would succeed quite spectacularly. He introduced a more flowing brand of football and four straight wins at the end of his first full season in charge saw Palace claim third spot and with it promotion to Division Two.

> *Our development at youth level convinces me that in two or three years' time we are going to have an exceptional side here at Selhurst – not only a team capable of getting into the First Division but one which will stay there and be a power.*
>
> Terry Venables, April 1977

–LEGENDS–

Peter Taylor

Peter Taylor made his Palace debut on 13th October 1973 at Oxford United, in a 1-1 draw in which Don Rogers scored, and would go on to spend three seasons at the club, making 142 appearances and scoring 39 goals. Taylor, twice the winner of the Player of the Year award (in 1973–74 and 1975–76), was a key figure in the dressing room in his playing days and went on to become yet another ex-Palace star who would one day manage the club. He won four caps for England – and would go on to manage the national side in a caretaker capacity, famously handing David Beckham the captain's armband for the first time in a game against Italy in 2000 – and scored two goals for his country. Taylor also represented the Three Lions at age-group level and scored for the Under-23s after just three minutes against Czechoslovakia in a game England won 3-1 . . . at Selhurst Park.

FOOTBALL –STATS–

Peter Taylor

Name: Peter Taylor

Born: 3rd January 1953 (Rochford)

Playing career: Southend United, Crystal Palace, Tottenham Hotspur, Leyton Orient, Oldham Athletic (loan), Exeter City; England

Position: Winger

Managerial career: Dartford, Southend United, Dover Athletic, England U-21, Gillingham, Leicester City, England (caretaker), Brighton & Hove Albion, Hull City, England U-21, Crystal Palace, Stevenage Borough, Wycombe Wanderers, Bradford City, Bahrain, England U-20

Palace appearances: 142 (1973–77)

Palace goals: 39

England appearances: 4

England goals: 2

> Peter's favourite trick was to walk into a packed hotel – and they were very grand then – storm into the restaurant, trip himself up and go flying all over the place. We'd run to pick him up and he'd be saying, 'It's all right lads, I'm okay'. He liked to have the biggest pudding ever, piled high and he'd suddenly fall face first into it and come up screaming, 'Who done that?' And everybody would be looking.
>
> Jim Cannon

> A fantastic bloke and a great character. He used to do impressions of Norman Wisdom and Tommy Cooper – that's what made me start doing them. When we were travelling up for my debut, I was on the coach and he was sitting opposite me. I looked at him all of a sudden and he mouthed, 'I love you'. I was young and mortified.
>
> Kenny Sansom

I would say to any kid, 'Go to Crystal Palace, because you will go there and you will be looked after and your family will be as well'. Crystal Palace is the best club I could ever have signed for as an apprentice. I don't think I could fault the club in any way.

Kenny Sansom

Kenny Sansom was always mimicking.

Jim Cannon

–LEGENDS–

Kenny Sansom

For many football fans, Kenny Sansom is best remembered as an Arsenal and England legend but it is testimony to both the footballer and the man that he can quite rightly claim to have been a legend at more than one club. Sansom came through the ranks at Palace and made almost 200 appearances for the club before Terry Venables sold him across London to Arsenal in a deal which took striker Clive Allen the other way. He captained the youth teams in which he played at Palace and made his first-team debut aged just 16 when Malcolm Allison played him on the final day of the 1974–75 campaign, a 2-0 defeat away at Tranmere Rovers. It was 10 months before Sansom played again, this time in a 2-1 victory at Grimsby Town on 13th March 1976, and then after missing the next few games he was thrown into the starting XI for the final five games of the season and never looked back. He would go on to miss just one League game out of 156 after that as Palace progressed back to Division One, and he won the first seven of his 86 England caps in 1979 while an Eagles player. Sansom was twice voted Player of the Year, in 1976–77 and 1978–79.

FOOTBALL –STATS–

Kenny Sansom

Name: Kenny Sansom

Born: 26th September 1958 (Camberwell)

Playing career: Crystal Palace, Arsenal, Newcastle United, Queens Park Rangers, Coventry City, Everton, Brentford, Watford; England

Position: Left-back

Palace appearances: 197 (1974–80)

Palace goals: 4

England appearances: 86

England goals: 1

The 1977–78 campaign was one of consolidation for Palace following their promotion to Division Two. They had started well, with a 3-0 victory at Millwall, thanks to goals from Ian Evans, Vince Hilaire and Nick Chatterton, on the opening day of the season and followed that up with a 3-1 win over fellow Second Division new boys Mansfield. Rachid Harkouk (two) and Martin Hinshelwood got the goals that day. Sadly the victories became more sporadic after that fine start and they finished a respectable ninth after managing just five wins from the turn of the year.

Dave Swindlehurst and Tony Gale battle it out on 28th October 1977 in a 1-0 win for Fulham.

Jim Cannon and Terry Fenwick celebrate with Dave Swindlehurst after he scored the only goal in a 1-0 victory at home to Leyton Orient on 11th April 1978.

–LEGENDS–

Vince Hilaire

Vince Hilaire was another Palace young gun who rose through the junior ranks and made his first-team debut while still in his teens. Manager Terry Venables gave him his debut at 17 from the substitutes' bench in a 3-2 defeat at Lincoln City on 2nd March 1977 – a game in which Dave Swindlehurst and Steve Brennan scored for the visitors – and he would go on to make nearly 300 appearances for the club over the next eight years. The midfielder was hugely popular in the dressing room and often the man behind some of the best practical jokes.

FOOTBALL
–STATS–

Vince Hilaire

Name: Vince Hilaire

Born: 10th October 1959 (Forest Hill)

Playing career: Crystal Palace, San Jose Earthquakes (USA; loan), Luton Town, Portsmouth, Leeds United, Stoke City, Exeter City

Position: Midfielder

Palace appearances: 293 (1976–84)

Palace goals: 36

Hilaire does battle with Bryan 'Pop' Robson of West Ham United in a 1-1 draw at Upton Park on 18th November 1978. Mike Elwiss got the Palace goal.

Hilaire in typical full flight.

> "
> *Vince was the character of the team, a fantastic lad and a great dribbler. He'd beat six people then cross it behind the goal, but no-one cared because he was such a great lad. He was a tremendous character and a great team player. He just wanted to be liked and he was liked, very, very much.*
>
> Kenny Sansom
> "

Rachid Harkouk's goal on 11th May – the third in a 4-2 victory over Wrexham – earned him the plaudits in the following day's *Mirror* after Palace had completed that run of four wins on the bounce at the end of the 1976–77 campaign to give themselves a real chance of promotion. They lay third behind Mansfield Town and Brighton & Hove Albion, and when Mansfield won 1-0 away at Wrexham the following Saturday, Palace were once again on the up. Kenny Sansom, Jim Cannon and Ian Evans had all played every League match that season.

–LEGENDS–

John Burridge

Budgie is another man who isn't just a legend at Palace but a legend of the game, a man for whom the phrase 'more clubs than [insert any golfer's name here]' could well have been coined. He made first-team appearances for 18 teams – 15 of them League clubs – in England and Scotland, although at some point or other he was on the books of perhaps twice that many throughout his career. Palace were the third club on that vast list and, as at all the other teams he played for, his lively character endeared him greatly to the fans. Venables snapped him up from Aston Villa and his pre-match routines, which often included all sorts of gymnastics, sometimes involving the use of his goalposts, made him a hit with the Palace faithful and the TV cameras, who regularly showed footage of his repertoire.

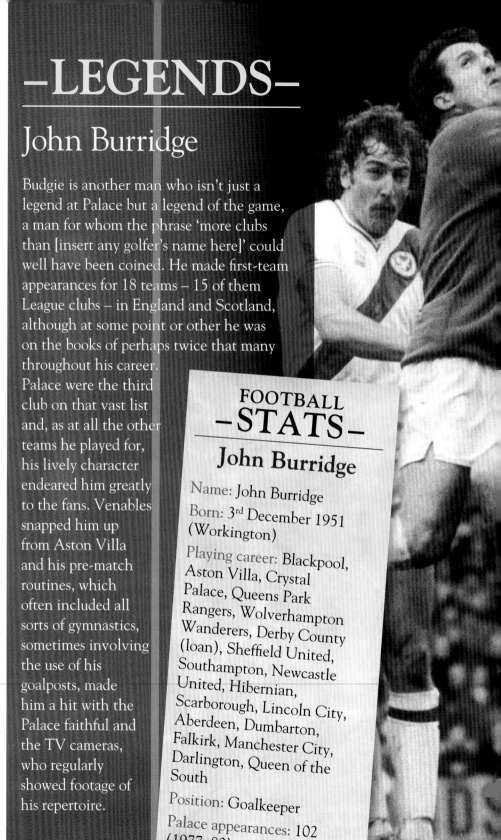

FOOTBALL –STATS–

John Burridge

Name: John Burridge

Born: 3rd December 1951 (Workington)

Playing career: Blackpool, Aston Villa, Crystal Palace, Queens Park Rangers, Wolverhampton Wanderers, Derby County (loan), Sheffield United, Southampton, Newcastle United, Hibernian, Scarborough, Lincoln City, Aberdeen, Dumbarton, Falkirk, Manchester City, Darlington, Queen of the South

Position: Goalkeeper

Palace appearances: 102 (1977–80)

ABOVE & RIGHT: Burridge indulges in some typical pre-match tomfoolery in August 1978.

LEFT: As well as the amusing antics, Burridge's longevity was all the proof required to show that there was also a highly professional side to his game. Here he punches clear under serious pressure from Liverpool's David Johnson with Jim Cannon trying to help out. This match, a Division One fixture on 26th April 1980, ended 0-0.

"John Burridge, famous for his warm-up routines and exaggerated muscle development exercises, [was] hilarious. Everybody knows what John was like – a complete nutter."

Jim Cannon

Palace's return to the top flight was secured on 11th May 1979 when a 2-0 victory over Burnley in front of 51,482 spectators at Selhurst Park – still the record attendance – saw them claim the Division Two crown from arch-rivals Brighton & Hove Albion in second place. Ian Walsh and Dave Swindlehurst got the goals for Terry Venables' side on that memorable day. Swindlehurst was another junior who went on to become a first-team regular and scored 81 goals in 276 games in all competitions for the club. His goals provided vital contributions to the promotions in 1976–77 and again in the 1978–79 season, when he hit 14 in the League to finish top scorer. Swindlehurst continued to score goals in the top flight as well, bagging seven in 21 games, and that tally was enough to make him Palace's leading goalscorer in the League again that season, despite the fact he was sold to Derby County for £400,000 – a record buy for the Rams at the time – in February 1980.

LEFT Swindlehurst in action against Arsenal on 10th November 1979, a 1-0 home win in which he scored.

RIGHT Scoring Palace's first goal in a 4-1 victory over Ipswich with an acrobatic effort on 29th September 1979.

BELOW Ian Walsh and Swindlehurst celebrate their goals in the 2-0 victory over Burnley which secured top spot for Palace on 11th May 1979 and sent them up into Division One.

> *That game against Burnley in front of nearly 52,000 people . . . that has to be the stand-out memory of my time at Palace. My debut was special and so was the Youth Cup final, but the Burnley game . . . It was mobbed. We were trying to run off the pitch and we got in the directors' area. We were in the directors' area and we all came out and clapped the fans because we couldn't get on the pitch. All the fans were singing for Palace and the players' names, and after 15 minutes we thought, 'That's enough'. We went back in, and one of the lads went, 'I want some more of that', so we ran back out and they were still there. It was a fantastic night.*
>
> Kenny Sansom

141

International Bright Young Things

Manager Terry Venables had put together a team of real talent and, naturally, international recognition followed for several of his stars. Jim Cannon of Scotland, Peter Nicholas of Wales, Jerry Murphy of the Republic of Ireland, and England's Kenny Sansom pose on 5th May 1979 ahead of a round of international fixtures.

Palace's New Hair-os

Promotion back to the big league meant Venables had some money to spend and he wasn't afraid to do just that. Twice he broke the club's transfer record before the season had started, first snapping up Gerry Francis from Queens Park Rangers for £465,000 and then going in for Mike Flanagan from Charlton for £650,000. The pair posed for snappers at the club's pre-season photocall ahead of that 1979–80 campaign.

Palace made a fine start to life in Division One, with three draws – against Manchester City, Southampton and Middlesbrough – preceding a 4-0 hammering of Derby County at home in which Mike Flanagan (with two), Peter Nicholas and Dave Swindlehurst all scored. Another draw against Wolves followed and, on the back of that result, there came further wins against Aston Villa, Stoke City and Ipswich Town, then a draw against Tottenham Hotspur before finally, at the hands of Southampton, Venables' side tasted defeat. During that run, Palace even sat pretty at the summit of English football . . . albeit for one week only at the end of September. It was an incredible feeling nonetheless and further proof of just how far the club had come.

BELOW: Kenny Sansom goes in on Arsenal's Frank Stapleton in a 1-1 draw at Highbury on 22nd March 1980. (Bottom) Sansom, Gerry Francis and Vince Hilaire join Dave Swindlehurst to celebrate his strike that day.

LEFT: Steve Kember in action against Manchester City on 3rd November 1979. Ian Walsh scored both the goals in the 2-0 home victory that day.

145

It was England's greatest goalscorer turned TV pundit Jimmy Greaves who dubbed Palace's young side the "Team of the Eighties". Terry Venables brought through a group of youngsters who knew each other's game inside out and combined them with established pros such as Jim Cannon and John Burridge to create a formidable team. Sadly, the team was broken up sooner

JOHN BURRIDGE

We used to take sleeping tablets and we'd give him Anadin, something like that instead, and he'd still go to sleep. He was a good character, always good fun and a great pro. Any youngsters who needed any help, he would help them out with an extra little bit of shooting for them, anything like that.

JIM CANNON

Jim was just Jim. Straight-lined, every game you'd get the same sort of performance. You talk about consistency, he was the epitome of the word. I did say to Terry Neill, "Sign him", when I signed for Arsenal. Typical of Terry, he signed Peter Nicholas and completely blanked me.

BILLY GILBERT

Billy never wore pants or socks and still doesn't today. He used to say, 'I don't like pants, I don't like socks, I'm not wearing them'. That was Billy. He would kick his mum as well if it meant winning a game. Great character, good lad.

IAN EVANS

Famously, George Best broke his leg. As Ian was trying to clear the ball George left his studs there. He didn't mean it. Ian was great for free-kicks, he was about 6ft 4in so whenever we got a free-kick it'd be, "Ian, you ready?"

PETER NICHOLAS

He was the one who used to get stuck in. He was a bit like Bryan Robson in that sense. I remember him once famously kicking Ray Kennedy at Liverpool and when we played them in the replay Graeme Souness got him back. Nicko was one of the midfield players who got stuck in. You needed him in your team.

JERRY MURPHY

Great skill and had fantastic talent. He used to dribble really, really well. Great character and a nice lad off the pitch. He was always smart. The one thing about Murph was that he always dressed immaculately, on and off the pitch.

KENNY SANSOM

The best player ever to play for Crystal Palace . . . No, I had a fantastic time and was very, very fortunate that I could have gone to several clubs – Leeds offered a lot of money for me to sign as an apprentice when Brian Clough was manager and I turned it down – but I moved to Crystal Palace and it was the right move.

DAVE SWINDLEHURST

Swindy was a great centre-forward – someone you could hit from a full-back's point of view. As soon as Budgie rolled the ball to me, I was looking for Swindy and he was always available. If you were in trouble you'd hit a cross to him knowing he'd hold it up. I think maybe I had a moustache because of him. His was horrible and mine was as well.

VINCE HILAIRE

His memory of the game was amazing. If you wanted to remember something about a certain game you'd ring him and he would tell you. Always wore different coloured socks to his trousers and we used to slaughter him for it. Black trousers and blue socks. He'd say, "I get dressed in the dark". I'd say, "Well turn the light on then". Every day he'd come in with the weirdest socks.

than anyone could have imagined and they were unable to live up to their moniker, but they will forever be remembered by those Palace fans fortunate enough to have seen them. Kenny Sansom, the team's left-back, dishes the dirt on his old pals . . .

BARRY SILKMAN

There was one day when he wore rubber studs and Terry Venables said to him, "If you pull out of a tackle, you're off". He should have worn studs but went for rubbers and I think in the second half he pulled out of a tackle and Terry took him off. I'm almost certain. He definitely gave him a telling-off. Very skilful player, could pass and cross, an intelligent player and a good lad.

MIKE ELWISS

Came in late, another centre-forward who was very similar to Swindy. He would always demand the ball as well, which I think is important. Unfortunately he was the one who had to room with John Burridge. He spoke in his sleep, Budgie, so that was Mike's punishment. I think Mike was the one who said, "Give me some Anadin to give to him".

TONY SEALEY

I didn't play a lot with Tony, a couple of times at best. He was very, very quick and used his pace. Terry used to tell him to use his pace and not worry about anything else, then tell us to get it in behind the full-back for him.

IAN WALSH

A fantastic centre-forward and he loved himself. Greatly. But not in a bad way, he was just a character and would lead with his ability which was very important. He was a team player as well, Walshy, and in the box he would score goals if you gave him a chance.

STEVE LOVELL

Only a kid when he came in, but brave as anything and would do anything to help the team. If you needed someone to make a tackle, he would make it. He'd never moan but he would wind people up if they weren't playing well, say, "Come on", and gee them up.

NICK CHATTERTON

Could run all day and never stop, and his dad was the groundsman. The thing he was famous for was that he lived down south, so when we were walking off the training pitch and heading for the showers he'd already be in his car and off – gone. He used to sprint off and he'd be in his car before we'd reached the hut.

PAUL HINSHELWOOD

He'd always be first in the running when we used to go to the Crystal Palace athletics track for training. Always a great lad and a great team player.

TERRY FENWICK

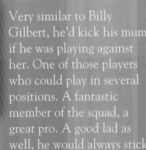

Very similar to Billy Gilbert, he'd kick his mum if he was playing against her. One of those players who could play in several positions. A fantastic member of the squad, a great pro. A good lad as well, he would always stick up for his team-mates.

A week after that game against Arsenal, Manchester United were the visitors to Selhurst Park as games against the big guns came thick and fast. And in the United side that day was a certain midfielder by the name of Steve Coppell, a man who would go on to become a true Palace legend as well.

Coppell makes a challenge at a ground that would one day become his home from home. United won the game, which took place on 29th March 1980, 2-0.

148

The final home game of the season saw Palace play out a 0-0 draw with Liverpool on 26th April 1980. A week later, Venables' side travelled to the City Ground for a game against Nottingham Forest and a 4-0 drubbing that day completed a disappointing run of just one win and four draws in their final 10 games. Still, finishing 13th was very respectable for Palace on their return to Division One.

'Supersub' David Fairclough of Liverpool is challenged by Palace's Terry Boyle. The Welshman spent four years at Selhurst Park from 1977–81, making 28 appearances and scoring twice.

As the *Mirror* reported on 13th August 1980, there was much coming and going between Arsenal and Crystal Palace, with left-back Kenny Sansom, to his surprise, heading to Highbury and striker Clive Allen going in the opposite direction. The pair were both valued at £1 million, with Palace boss Terry Venables also paying £400,000 for Arsenal's reserve goalkeeper Paul Barron.

LEFT: Million-pound-men Allen (left) and Sansom toast their swap moves across London.

RIGHT: Allen in action for Palace against Leeds United at Elland Road on 25th October 1980. The visitors lost the game 1-0.

All Change in the Manager's Office

It wasn't just Sansom and Allen on the move at that time as the start of the Eighties signalled another period of significant change at the club. The 1980–81 season started terribly with just one win and nine defeats in Palace's opening 10 games and, on 14th October, Venables left suddenly to take over at Division Two side Queens Park Rangers. Ernie Walley took over until 1st December and he was replaced by former manager Malcolm Allison. In late January 1981, Ron Noades bought the club and his arrival coincided with Allison's departure and Dario Gradi's installment as manager.

LEFT Terry Venables is happy with his side's work at the end of a goalless home draw with Liverpool on 26th May 1980, less than five months before his departure.

RIGHT Malcolm Allison, pictured here five years earlier during his first spell as Palace manager with Bunny Girl Serena Williams, returned for a second, short-lived stint.

RIGHT Dario Gradi was the man brought in by new chairman and owner Ron Noades.

153

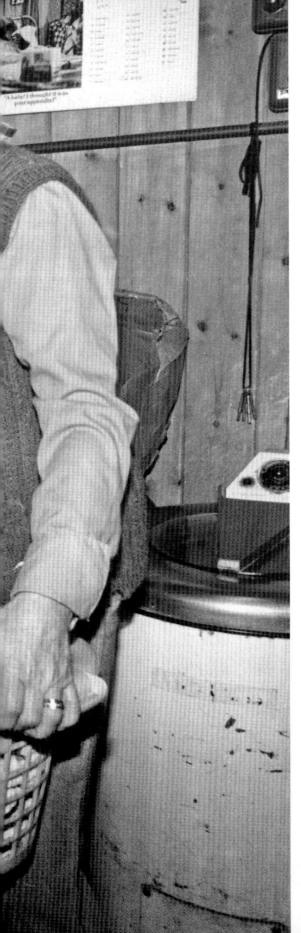

The real heroes of any club, those who are there long before and long after most players, managers and chairmen have come and gone, are those who work behind the scenes to get kits crisp and clean and (above) terraces swept, among the many other jobs. At Palace that was, and still is, no different. The chores were being done in this photograph (left) ahead of the visit of Manchester United on 1st November 1980 and the hard work was all worthwhile as the lads did the business out on the pitch as well, recording a 1-0 victory thanks to a goal from Peter Nicholas. Jim Cannon and Bill Smilie (right) give themselves a rub down after the game . . . and create a whole machine-load's more work for the girls. Sadly, that result was one of the few highlights of a rollercoaster season, and the changes on and off the field ended with Palace finishing bottom of Division One and returning to the second tier after just two seasons back at the top level.

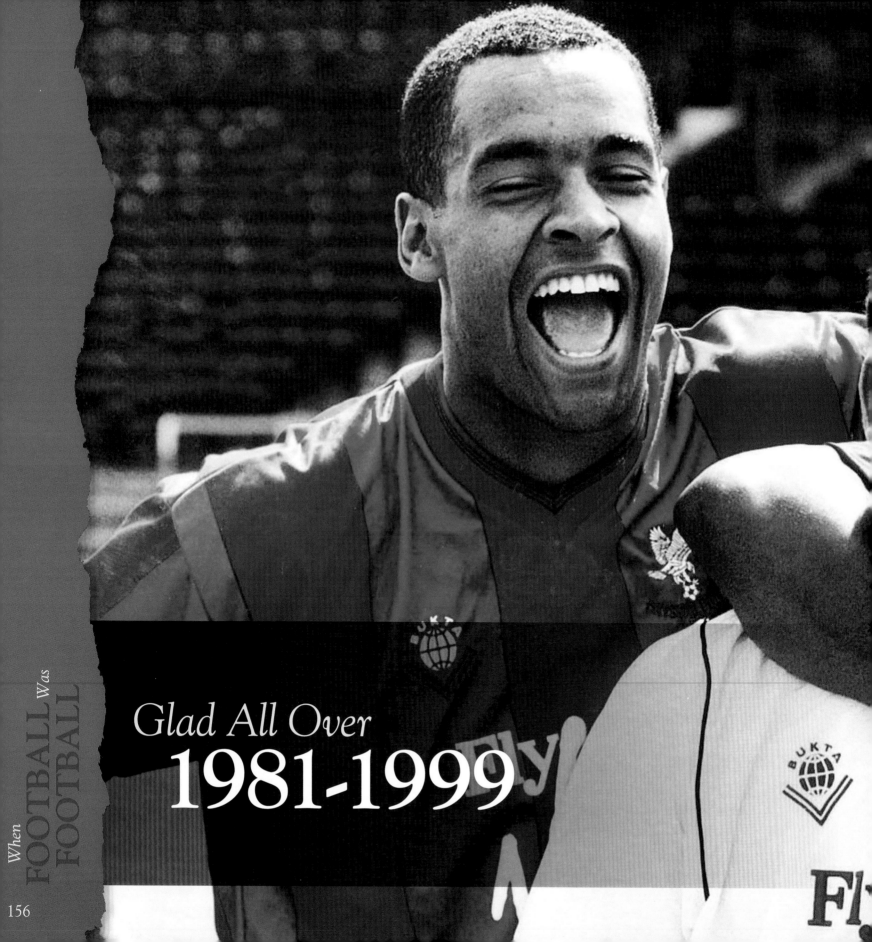

Glad All Over
1981-1999

Star strikers Mark Bright and Ian Wright flank manager Steve Coppell at Selhurst Park in 1989.

1981 Ron Noades arrives as chairman in January but Palace finish 22nd and drop back into Division Two. **1988** Jim Cannon makes his last appearance for the club after 15 years' service. The defender played 660 games for Palace, which remains a club record. **1989** Ian Wright and Mark Bright established themselves as one of the most dangerous strike partnerships in Division Two and, after eight years in the second tier, their goals help Steve Coppell's side to promotion. A strike apiece from Wright and Bright, and a penalty from Dave Madden, give the Eagles a 3-0 win over Blackburn Rovers in the play-off final. **1990** A record 9-0 League defeat by Liverpool early in the campaign isn't exactly the sort of result Palace had hoped for when they got back to the top flight, but they survive the season. More memorably, the club reaches the FA Cup final against Manchester United, recording a 3-3 draw before losing the replay 1-0. **1991** The club finish third in Division One and beat Everton at Wembley to win the Zenith Data Systems Cup. **1993** Palace can't beat the drop and are relegated from the Premier League after losing against Arsenal at Highbury on the final day of the season. **1994** It is only a short stay in the First Division, though, with the club returning to the Premier League at the first attempt by winning the title. **1995** The restructuring of the Premier League costs Palace dear. They finish fourth from bottom but it's not good enough to save them with the top flight reduced to a 20-team competition. It's a good season in both the FA Cup and League Cup, however, with the last four reached in both competitions. **1997** David Hopkin scores the only goal of the game to take Palace back into the big time as Sheffield United are beaten in the First Division play-off final. **1998** The Eagles continue to yo-yo between the top two divisions and, after finishing bottom of the Premier League, are relegated to Division One. Mark Goldberg takes over the club and becomes chairman, but the 1998–99 season ends with financial problems and the business in the hands of administrators.

RIGHT Local businessman Ron Noades bought the club in January 1981 and takes a look around the Selhurst Park premises on day one of his tenure. Noades would eventually sell the club, but not the ground, to Mark Goldberg for £22 million in 1998.

Palace won just one game in Division One following Dario Gradi's arrival on 26th January 1980 – they beat Birmingham City 3-1, with two goals from Tommy Langley and one from Steve Lovell on 11th April – and, after a mixed start to the following campaign in Division Two and just 10 months after Gradi's appointment, Noades decided it was time for a change of manager. Former fans' favourite Steve Kember was handed the caretaker manager's role.

This picture (far left) of new boss Kember in the Palace dugout appeared in the *Sunday People* in November 1981. Just a few weeks later, it didn't matter how senior anyone was at the club, they were needed to clear the pitch of snow to get a League Cup fourth-round clash with West Brom on at Selhurst Park a day or two later. Perhaps the chaps shouldn't have bothered, though; the Baggies won 3-1 with Tommy Langley grabbing the consolation goal.

Kember remained in charge for the rest of the 1981–82 season but chairman Noades, controversially, brought in former England ace Alan Mullery ahead of the new campaign. It was an interesting appointment. Mullery had been in charge of Brighton & Hove Albion during the 1976–77 season when the rivalry between the two clubs began. He and Terry Venables, who was in charge of Palace and, like Mullery, had only taken over his club that summer, had been Tottenham team-mates a decade earlier and, by the end of that season, the friendly competition between the two of them had escalated into a bitter rivalry between the two sets of supporters.

The two clubs met five times in the 1976–77 season – an FA Cup first-round match needing two replays – and it was after the second replay, which Palace won, that the acrimony between the two clubs really exploded. Mullery had a run-in with Palace fans after one of them, he alleged, threw a cup of coffee over him. His response was to throw the change from his pocket to the floor in front of them and say, "That's all you're worth, Crystal Palace". Unsurprisingly, Mullery's first season in charge was a difficult one, with the battle for Division Two survival, one which involved almost half of the teams in the League, going right down to the final day of the season. Palace survived thanks to a 1-0 victory at Burnley on 18th May 1983. Four teams, including Palace, finished on 48 points, two on 47 and the relegated three, Rotherham United, Burnley and Bolton Wanderers, went down with 45, 44 and 44 points respectively.

ABOVE: Alan Mullery was never slow to get his point across and, in December 1982, first-team favourites Jim Cannon and Vince Hilaire were treated to a few words of his wisdom.

LEFT: Ian Edwards celebrates his goal in the 1-0 win against Burnley on the final game of the 1982–83 season, a goal which kept Palace up by the skin of their teeth.

The following season again proved a struggle for Mullery and his players, the club finishing sixth from bottom of Division Two, and there would be another change of manager. There wasn't much to shout about in the FA and League Cups, either, with Peterborough knocking Palace out of the latter competition in the first round and West Ham proving a step too far in the other after Leicester City had been beaten in the third round. Palace drew the first game at Selhurst Park 1-1, with Andy McCullough getting the goal, but the Hammers won the replay on 31st January 1984, 2-0.

Former Palace hero Dave Swindlehurst (not in picture) beats keeper George Wood to earn West Ham a 1-1 draw on his old stamping ground on 28th January 1984. West Ham won the replay, three days later, 2-0.

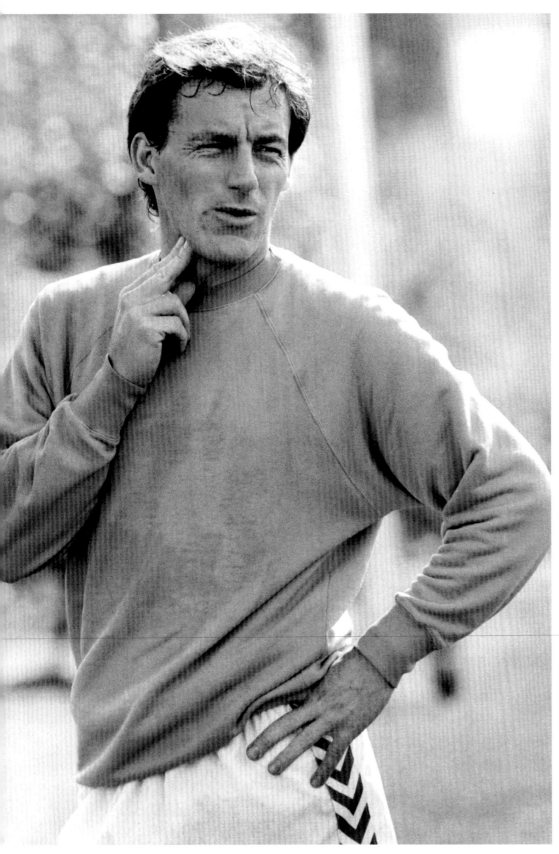

Coppell's Club

Palace fans did not know it at the time, of course, but an international fixture between England and Hungary at Wembley in November 1981 would have an effect on the club which, while not immediate, would certainly be long-lasting. Steve Coppell, the Manchester United midfielder, sustained an injury during that game from which he would never fully recover and, in 1983, he was forced to call time on his playing career. A year later, following a meeting with Palace chairman Ron Noades, the then 28-year-old was handed the manager's

job at Selhurst Park and an Eagles legend was in the making. Coppell, with an eye for young and untested talent, would rebuild the team and put together a squad which would enjoy some of, if not *the*, most successful years in the club's history. He would spend nine years at the helm during that first spell in charge – he had four in total as well as becoming director of football – and was a figurehead for the Supporters' Trust when the club went into administration.

On the training pitch in October 1987 (left); flanked by Jim Cannon, Micky Droy and George Wood at Palace's training ground on 24th September 1986 (below); and assuming the role of head chef ahead of the FA Cup final in May 1990 (right).

–LEGENDS–

Ian Wright and Mark Bright

Ian Wright, a former plasterer's labourer, was snapped up by Steve Coppell from non-League Greenwich Borough in the summer of 1985 and what an acquisition he would prove to be. Aged just 21 and still a raw talent, Wright scored nine goals in his first season at Palace and would go on to become one of the most prolific goalscorers in the club's history with 117 in 277 appearances. Little more than a year after Wright's arrival, Coppell signed 24-year-old Mark Bright from Leicester City and the pair would become the most famous double-act in the club's history. They formed a lethal partnership and scored goals for fun both in Division Two and, after firing Palace to promotion, in Division One, famously helping the club finish third in the top flight in the 1990–91 campaign. Bright's statistics at Palace – 113 goals in 286 appearances – were remarkably similar to Wright's, but surprisingly, and unlike his strike partner, an England call-up was never forthcoming. Wright, who scored twice for Palace in the FA Cup final against Manchester United in 1990, a game which ended 3-3 with United winning the replay, left for Arsenal in 1991 for a fee of £2.5 million, while Bright joined Sheffield Wednesday a year later.

FOOTBALL –STATS–

Ian Wright

Name: Ian Wright

Born: 3rd November 1963 (Woolwich)

Playing career: Crystal Palace, Arsenal, West Ham United, Nottingham Forest (loan), Celtic, Burnley; England

Position: Striker

Palace appearances: 277 (1985–91)

Palace goals: 117

England appearances: 33

England goals: 9

Ian Wright celebrates one of his two goals in the 4-1 victory over Everton in the Zenith Data Systems Cup at Wembley on 7th April 1991 and cadges a lift from strike partner Bright at the launch of Palace's tie-in with new sponsors Tulip Computers just a few days later.

FOOTBALL
—STATS—
Mark Bright

Name: Mark Bright

Born: 6th June 1962 (Stoke-on-Trent)

Playing career: Port Vale, Leicester City, Crystal Palace, Sheffield Wednesday, Millwall (loan), Sion (Switzerland), Charlton Athletic

Position: Striker

Palace appearances: 286 (1986–92)

Palace goals: 113

" *Ian and Mark had an almost telepathic understanding.*

Gary O'Reilly "

Mark Bright in action in the FA Cup semi-final against Liverpool at Villa Park on 8th April 1990. Bright scored Palace's first goal in the 4-3 victory.

167

FA Cup Semi-final

Coppell's effect on Palace was huge and, after a mid-table finish in his first season, the club ended the following three Division Two campaigns in fifth, sixth and sixth respectively. It was clear, though, that he was building another special Palace team and, at the end of the decade, things really came together. Palace finished third in the 1988–89 season, behind Chelsea and Manchester City, and followed those two clubs into the top flight with a play-off final victory over Blackburn, winning 4-3 on aggregate. What a memorable couple of years those which followed would prove to be. In the League, Palace consolidated and finished the campaign sixth from bottom to retain their status, but it was their fortunes in the FA Cup for which the season will always be recalled. Palace had long enjoyed good fortunes in cup matches but a magical run to the semi-finals saw them on the brink of reaching their first FA Cup final. They were drawn against Liverpool – the runaway League leaders and a team which had already beaten Palace 9-0 and 2-0 that season – at Villa Park on 8th April 1990 and they recorded an incredible 4-3 victory, after extra-time and thanks to goals from Mark Bright, Gary O'Reilly, Andy Gray and Alan Pardew. Liverpool, who had led twice, would go on to win the League quite comfortably that year, reinforcing just what a spectacular victory it had been.

RIGHT: Alan Pardew wheels away in delight after scoring Palace's fourth goal, sparking mass delirium among the Palace players and ranks and leading to some wonderful scenes on the pitch after the game.

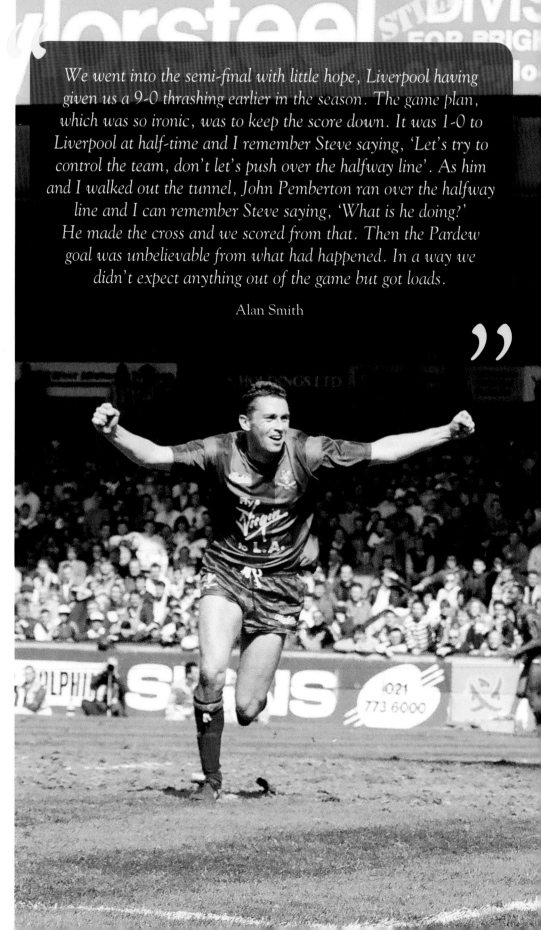

"We went into the semi-final with little hope, Liverpool having given us a 9-0 thrashing earlier in the season. The game plan, which was so ironic, was to keep the score down. It was 1-0 to Liverpool at half-time and I remember Steve saying, 'Let's try to control the team, don't let's push over the halfway line'. As him and I walked out the tunnel, John Pemberton ran over the halfway line and I can remember Steve saying, 'What is he doing?' He made the cross and we scored from that. Then the Pardew goal was unbelievable from what had happened. In a way we didn't expect anything out of the game but got loads."

Alan Smith

–LEGENDS–

Geoff Thomas

Steve Coppell paid £50,000 to take tough-tackling midfielder Geoff Thomas to Palace from Crewe in 1987 and he went on to captain the club as well as win the Player of the Year award twice. He was captain at Wembley in the FA Cup final and became an England international while a player at Selhurst Park. A decade after leaving Palace in 1993, Thomas was diagnosed with leukaemia but he made a successful recovery and dedicates much of his time now to raising money for The Geoff Thomas Foundation. Thomas won the BBC's Sports Personality of the Year Helen Rollason Award, an award given in honour of outstanding achievement in the face of adversity, after completing the route of the 2005 Tour de France just a few days before the race itself and was voted into Palace's Centenary XI by fans the same year.

RIGHT: Thomas and Tottenham's Paul Stewart clash at White Hart Lane on 16th February 1992. Palace won the game 1-0 thanks to an Eddie McGoldrick goal.

FOOTBALL –STATS–

Geoff Thomas

Name: Geoff Thomas

Born: 5th August 1964 (Manchester)

Playing career: Rochdale, Crewe Alexandra, Crystal Palace, Wolverhampton Wanderers, Nottingham Forest, Barnsley, Notts County, Crewe Alexandra; England

Position: Midfielder

Palace appearances: 249 (1987–93)

Palace goals: 35

England appearances: 9

RIGHT: Thomas thanks the supporters after the 3-0 victory over Manchester United on 11th May which brought down the curtain at home on the 1990–91 campaign.

BELOW RIGHT: Thomas, second right, regularly rides his bike for charity and is pictured here with a group of fellow celebrities ahead of the *Daily Mirror*'s Great Manchester Cycle in 2012.

Que sera, sera, whatever will be, will be, we're going to Wem-ber-lee . . .
How Palace reached the Twin Towers:

Third round, 6th January:
Crystal Palace 2 Portsmouth 1
(Gray (pen), Thomas)

Fourth round, 27th January:
Crystal Palace 4 Huddersfield 0
(Hopkins, Lewis (own goal), Bright, Salako)

Fifth round, 17th February:
Crystal Palace 1 Rochdale 0
(Barber)

Quarter-final, 10th March:
Cambridge United 0 Crystal Palace 1
(Thomas)

Semi-final, 8th April (at Villa Park):
Crystal Palace 4 Liverpool 3 *aet
(Bright, O'Reilly, Gray, Pardew)

The iconic image of the 1990 FA Cup final as, suited and booted, Palace stars get a feel of the famous Wembley turf. From left to right, they are: John Salako, Richard Shaw, Ian Wright, Andy Gray, Alex Dyer and Mark Bright.

The FA Cup final which took place on 12th May 1990 will live long in the memories of English football fans in general and not just those of the two teams – Palace and Manchester United – who contested it. It was some occasion and some game, with twists and turns, and excitement throughout. Palace took the lead through Gary O'Reilly's header, although United were level before half-time thanks to a Bryan Robson goal. Mark Hughes then put United ahead after the break but the introduction of Ian Wright, back from a broken leg, as a substitute was inspired from manager Steve Coppell and the striker hauled his side level three minutes after entering the fray. That goal forced extra-time and Palace reclaimed the lead early on with Wright bagging his second of the day. Sadly, though, United weren't finished either, and Hughes scored his second of the game to force a replay back at Wembley five days later, which the men from Old Trafford won 1-0.

Final Teams

CRYSTAL PALACE: Martyn, Pemberton, Shaw, Gray, O'Reilly, Thorn, Barber, Thomas, Bright, Salako, Pardew. **Substitutes:** Wright, Madden.

MANCHESTER UNITED: Leighton*, Ince, Martin, Bruce, Phelan, Pallister, Robson, Webb, McClair, Hughes, Wallace. **Substitutes:** Robins, Blackmore.

* Only one change was made to the starting line-ups for the replay at Wembley on 17th May, with
  Jim Leighton replaced by Les Sealey in goal for Manchester United.

> "
> *The final was phenomenal,*
> *with Wrighty coming off the bench.*
> *He had been having treatment from a*
> *faith healer and that's how we got him*
> *out there. He was such a big part of*
> *what we were about. He helped us win*
> *games we should never have won.*
>
> Alan Smith
> "

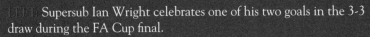

LEFT: Supersub Ian Wright celebrates one of his two goals in the 3-3 draw during the FA Cup final.

BELOW: Andy Gray can't stop Clayton Blackmore getting to the ball while Gary O'Reilly goes shoulder-to-shoulder with Mark Hughes.

–LEGENDS–

Nigel Martyn

Nigel Martyn famously became the first £1 million goalkeeper in Britain when Palace signed him from Bristol Rovers in 1989 and it was during his seven seasons at Selhurst Park that he won the first of his 23 England caps. He proved seriously good value for money during that time and Palace showed what a great piece of business he was when they sold him to Leeds for £2.5 million. Martyn was voted into the Centenary XI as the best goalkeeper in the club's history.

FOOTBALL –STATS–

Nigel Martyn

Name: Nigel Martyn

Born: 11th August 1966 (St Austell)

Playing career: Bristol Rovers, Crystal Palace, Leeds United, Everton; England

Position: Goalkeeper

Palace appearances: 349 (1989–96)

England appearances: 23

Martyn in action (left) during a 1-0 victory over Aston Villa at Selhurst Park on 24th March 1990 – Garry Thompson got the goal that day – and (above and below) during and after the FA Cup semi-final win against Liverpool.

Alan Pardew was a key player for Palace during the promotion-winning campaign of 1988–89 and again in Division One the following season. He will forever be remembered by Palace fans for scoring the winning goal in the FA Cup semi-final against Liverpool. Pardew left the club in 1991 to join Charlton Athletic and would later go on to be a successful manager at Reading, West Ham United, Charlton, Southampton and Newcastle United.

Pardew celebrates after scoring in a 2-2 Division One draw with Manchester City in the final game of the 1989–90 season. Andy Gray was also on target for Palace that day.

Salako celebrates one of his two goals in the victory over United at Selhurst Park on 11th May 1991. Ian Wright scored Palace's other goal that day and is pictured (below), celebrating with the Zenith Data Systems Cup on 7th April after striking twice in the final.

Eagles Soar

The FA Cup final might not have ended quite how Palace wanted it to but the following season they took their cup heroics into the League campaign. Palace finished the season third in Division One, recording their highest-ever placing, behind Arsenal and Liverpool after winning 3-0 at home to Manchester United in the penultimate game of the season and beating Wimbledon 3-0, thanks to an Ian Wright hat-trick, in the Dons' last game at Plough Lane. Despite reaching the FA Cup final in the previous campaign, the Eagles went out of the competition at the first attempt, losing a third-round tie with Nottingham Forest, albeit after two replays. But while the Zenith Data Systems Cup might not have held the history and kudos of the world's oldest domestic cup competition, it still brought some silverware to the club and a great day out for the fans towards the end of the season. Palace beat Bristol City, Brighton & Hove Albion, Luton Town and Norwich City to reach the Wembley final against Everton on 7th April 1991 and a 4-1 win was achieved thanks to a goal apiece from Geoff Thomas and John Salako, and two from Ian Wright.

All good things come to an end, apparently, and the reign of Steve Coppell at Crystal Palace was no different. Division One was rebranded as the Premiership at the start of the 1992–93 campaign and, sadly for Palace, the history books will always show them to have been one of the three clubs relegated at the end of that first year, along with Middlesbrough and Nottingham Forest. It had been a nerve-shredding end to the season and a 3-0 defeat by Arsenal at Highbury condemned Palace to the drop on goal difference from Oldham, who had also finished on 49 points. It wasn't the first time Arsenal had inflicted heartache on the club that season – a 5-1 aggregate victory from the North London outfit dumping the Eagles out of the League Cup semi-finals. Coppell decided to step down at the end of the campaign and assistant Alan Smith was promoted to the top job.

RIGHT: Coppell takes his time to cast an eye over Selhurst Park on 22nd May 1993, having resigned at a press conference that day with chairman Ron Noades.

Steve's nature was always glass half-full, but in a good way, and I think that's why, if I can say so, we complemented each other.

Alan Smith

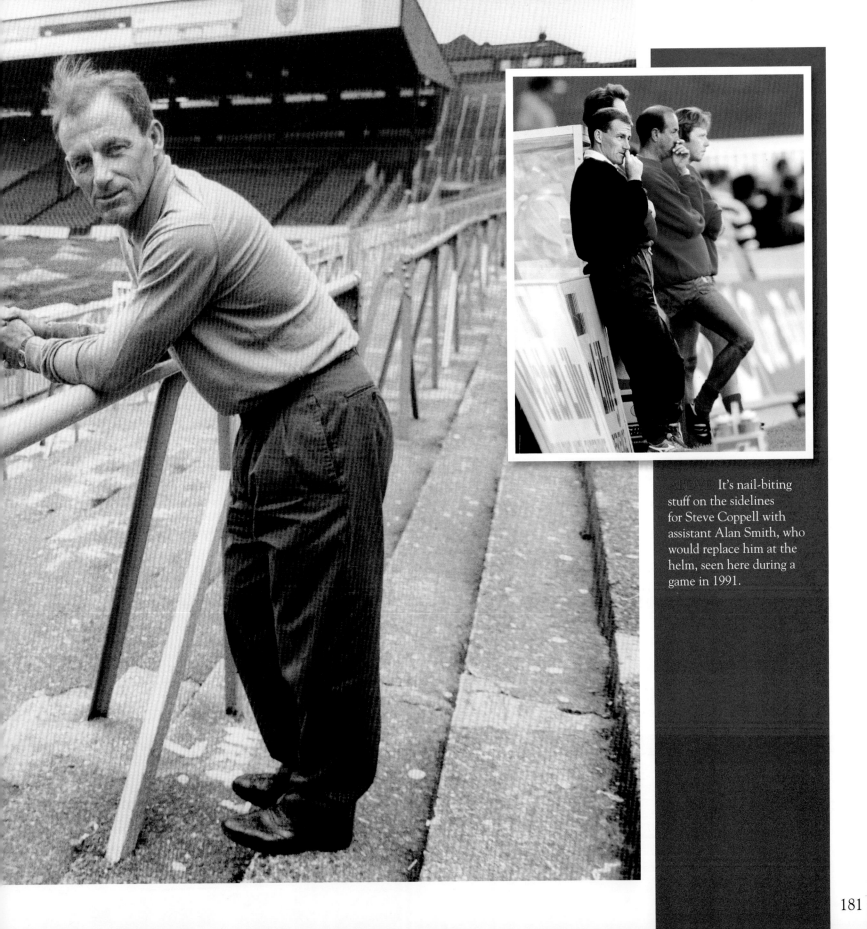

ABOVE: It's nail-biting stuff on the sidelines for Steve Coppell with assistant Alan Smith, who would replace him at the helm, seen here during a game in 1991.

Smith's promotion proved to be a smart move and he returned Palace to the top flight at the first attempt. They topped Division One, seven points ahead of second-placed Nottingham Forest, with goalkeeper Nigel Martyn and defenders Gareth Southgate and Chris Coleman assured all season, and Chris Armstrong leading from the front with 23 League goals. The Palace boss finally admitted to the *Mirror* on 11th April 1994 that he knew his side were going up.

Defender Richard Shaw tussles with former Palace favourite Mark Bright during a 1-0 defeat at Hillsborough by Sheffield Wednesday on 3rd December 1994. Bright had joined the Owls in 1992.

An Early Bath for Cantona

Palace's return to the big time was short-lived and cruelly so. The Premiership was reduced from 22 teams to 20 at the end of the 1994–95 campaign and Palace's finish, fourth from bottom despite amassing 45 points, meant they were down. The season, however, will always be best remembered not for relegation but for the quite remarkable incident which took place at Selhurst Park on 25th January 1995. Manchester United's flamboyant Frenchman Eric Cantona snapped after being sent off for a kick at defender Richard Shaw and launched himself over the advertising hoardings and into the crowd as he aimed a kung fu kick and a series of punches at Palace fan Matthew Simmons. Simmons was famously reported in one newspaper to have claimed Cantona reacted to him simply saying, "Off you go Cantona – it's an early bath for you", though those within earshot have suggested the language was far more industrial and, indeed, offensive than that. Either way, the whole episode will live long in the memory of every fan who watched football at the time. Cantona was banned for nine months and ordered to carry out 120 hours of community service. When given the opportunity to explain his actions at a press conference, Cantona famously said: "When the seagulls follow the trawler, it's because they think sardines will be thrown into the sea. Thank you very much."

The astonishing scenes at Selhurst Park the previous night made the front page news in the *Mirror* on 26th January 1995.

> *United had a phenomenal team. We looked at them before the game and they were a big team, they played in all black, they hadn't had a shave, they looked like hard men. Roy Keane, Paul Ince . . . I'd said to the lads that we had to match them physically and Richard Shaw took it literally, I think. And that was it. There was just relief on my mind to think Cantona wasn't going to be on the pitch for the rest of the game after the incident. There was a disbelief of what he had done in my mind.*
>
> Alan Smith

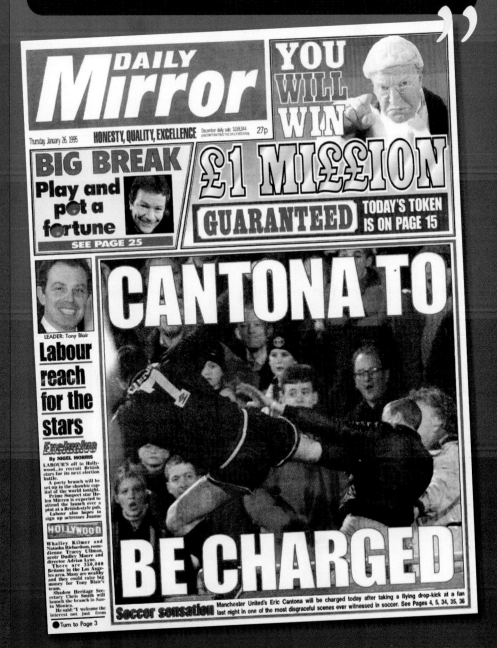

Ron Noades took the decision to relieve Alan Smith of his post the day after the 1994–95 season ended and Steve Coppell returned to the club as technical director with Ray Lewington and Peter Nicholas installed as caretaker managers. Dave Bassett took over full time from 8th February 1996. By the end of the season, Palace were third behind Sunderland and Derby County, and reached the play-off final after beating Charlton Athletic 2-1 and 1-0 in the two-legged semis. There was heartbreak in the final at Wembley, however, where Palace lost 2-1 to Leicester City, with Andy Roberts scoring the Eagles' goal.

ABOVE: George Ndah and Carl Veart enjoy the moment after the latter's goal in the play-off semi-final first leg against Charlton at The Valley. Kenny Brown scored Palace's first in that 2-1 victory and Ray Houghton got the only goal of the game in the second leg.

LEFT: Dave Bassett and Charlton manager Alan Curbishley enjoy a pint ahead of their sides' play-off semi-final clashes in May 1996.

Shipperley Shape

Neil Shipperley had two spells at Crystal Palace, scoring 20 goals in 61 games between 1996 and 1998, and eight in 41 from 2003 to 2005. His first season at the club saw him score 12 goals in 29 games and he helped them finish sixth, under the guidance first of Dave Bassett and, from February, Steve Coppell, who was reinstalled as manager. That finish meant Palace had reached the play-offs once more and Shipperley scored the opener against Wolverhampton Wanderers in the semi-final first leg. Dougie Freedman also scored in the 3-1 win and that result was enough to send them to the showpiece at Wembley, despite a 2-1 defeat in the second leg in which David Hopkin scored.

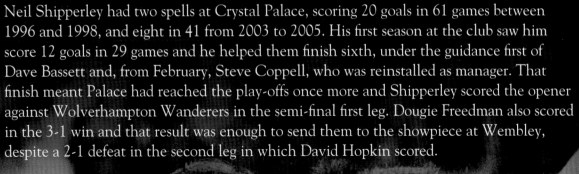

Dougie Freedman and David Hopkin join Neil Shipperley as he takes the acclaim from Palace fans following one of his two goals against Swindon Town at the County Ground on 27th April 1997. Palace won the game 2-0.

185

Palace fans, like most other sets of supporters, love players with flair, but hard-working footballers are perhaps treated with more reverence at Selhurst Park than at many other clubs. David Hopkin was another player who fitted that mould and the tenacious midfielder was a real hero on the terraces during the 1996–97 campaign. He was superb that season and, fittingly, it was the Scot's 90th-minute effort which gave Palace a 1-0 victory over Sheffield United at Wembley in the play-off final. It was a wonderful goal, a curling effort, and it buried the memories of the defeat by Leicester a year earlier to lift the Eagles back into the big time. Hopkin's status was immediately raised to cult hero . . . but he left to join Leeds just a few weeks later. In 2000, Hopkin returned to the club for another two-year spell and in total made 126 appearances in all competitions for Palace, scoring 33 goals. None, however, were as memorable as that stunner at Wembley.

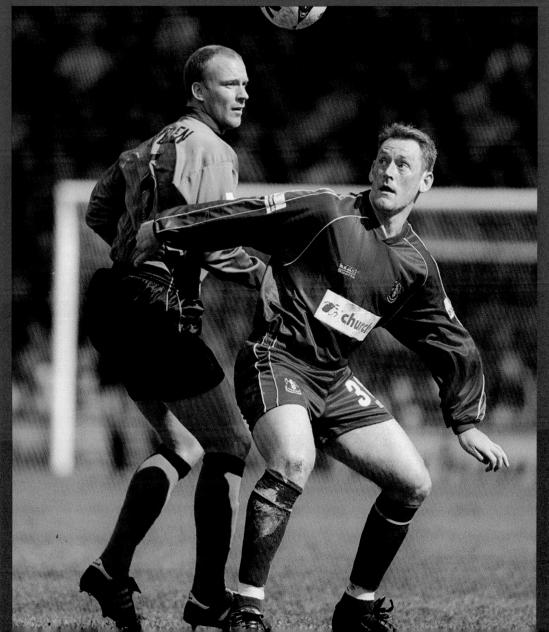

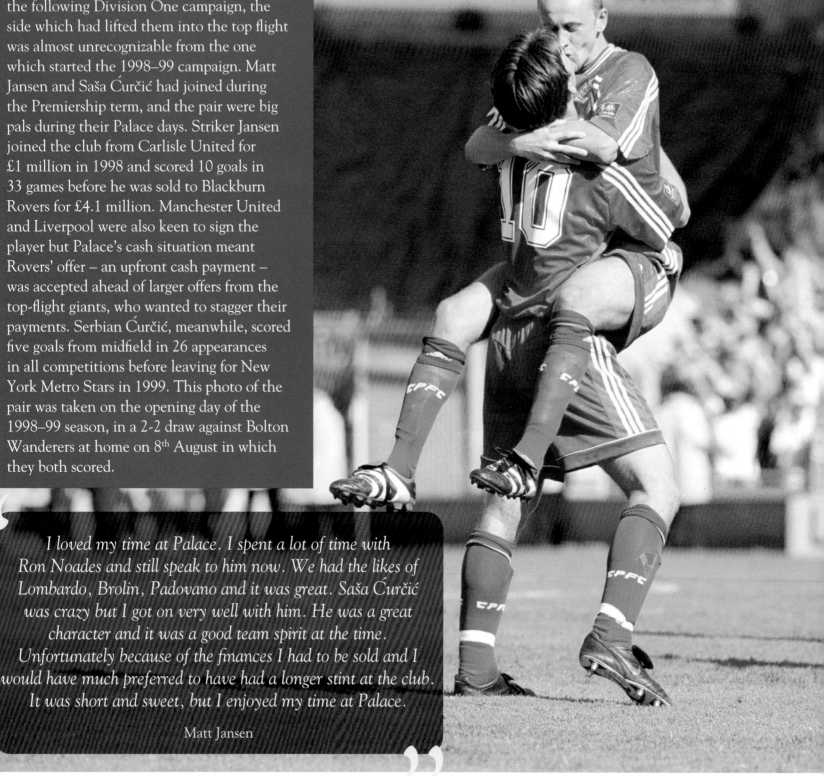

Palace's stay in the Premiership again lasted for just one season and when the club began the following Division One campaign, the side which had lifted them into the top flight was almost unrecognizable from the one which started the 1998–99 campaign. Matt Jansen and Saša Ćurčić had joined during the Premiership term, and the pair were big pals during their Palace days. Striker Jansen joined the club from Carlisle United for £1 million in 1998 and scored 10 goals in 33 games before he was sold to Blackburn Rovers for £4.1 million. Manchester United and Liverpool were also keen to sign the player but Palace's cash situation meant Rovers' offer – an upfront cash payment – was accepted ahead of larger offers from the top-flight giants, who wanted to stagger their payments. Serbian Ćurčić, meanwhile, scored five goals from midfield in 26 appearances in all competitions before leaving for New York Metro Stars in 1999. This photo of the pair was taken on the opening day of the 1998–99 season, in a 2-2 draw against Bolton Wanderers at home on 8th August in which they both scored.

"
I loved my time at Palace. I spent a lot of time with Ron Noades and still speak to him now. We had the likes of Lombardo, Brolin, Padovano and it was great. Saša Ćurčić was crazy but I got on very well with him. He was a great character and it was a good team spirit at the time. Unfortunately because of the finances I had to be sold and I would have much preferred to have had a longer stint at the club. It was short and sweet, but I enjoyed my time at Palace.
"

Matt Jansen

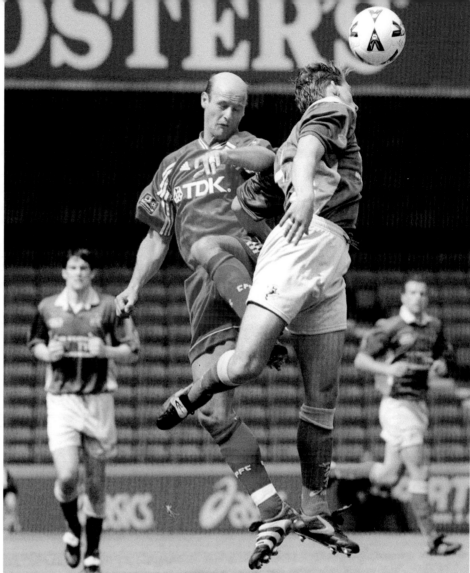

Attilio Lombardo was a huge hit with Palace fans during his stay between 1997 and 1999, joining from Juventus in his native Italy and immediately striking up a bond with the Selhurst Park faithful. He scored on his debut in a 2-1 win against Everton on 9th August and assumed cult status as one of the most gifted players ever to appear for the club. His ability saw him voted into the Centenary XI in 2005 and Lombardo was even installed as caretaker manager for six weeks during the ill-fated Premiership season of 1997–98, following Steve Coppell's departure, and before Ron Noades, Ray Lewington and Brian Sparrow took over for the last three matches. He endeared himself to the fans by sticking with the club despite relegation that season but further money problems led to his sale the following campaign. He left the club having scored 10 goals in 48 appearances, returning to his homeland to join Lazio.

ABOVE: Lombardo in action in a pre-season friendly against Millwall in August 1998.

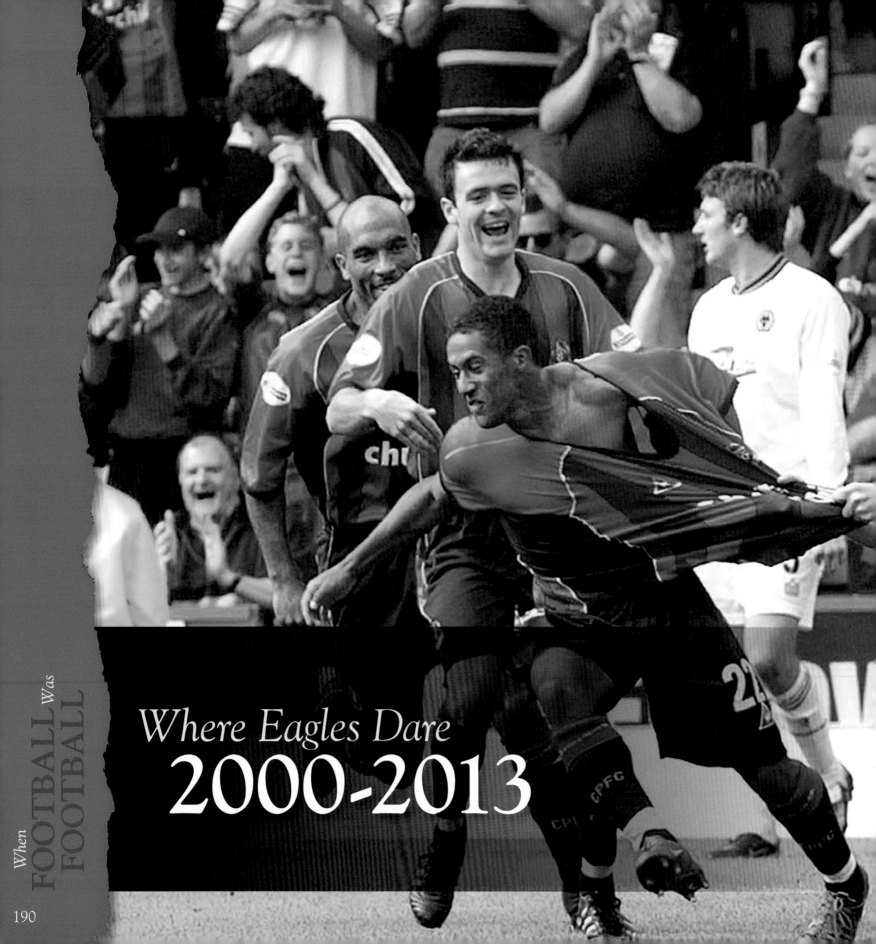

Where Eagles Dare
2000-2013

Andy Johnson gets to grips with Wayne Routledge after his goal in a 4-2 victory over Wolves on 14th September 2002. Dougie Freedman scored twice that day, once from the penalty spot, and Steven Thomson was also on the scoresheet.

2000 Simon Jordan takes control of the club and the Eagles finally come out of administration in July. Ex-manager Alan Smith is reinstalled as manager. Coach Steve Kember is put in temporary charge with two games of the 2000–01 season remaining and a win at Stockport on the final day of the season ensures the club retains its Division One status. **2003–04** Palace begin 2004 fourth from bottom in Division One but Iain Dowie's arrival as manager sparks an incredible run of results to lift the club into the play-offs. Sunderland are beaten on penalties as the club book their place in the showpiece final at the Millennium Stadium and Neil Shipperley becomes the latest Selhurst Park hero as he fires the goal which sends them back into the top flight. **2005** It's the same old story again this time out as the club are relegated after one of the most memorable last days in Premier League history. 'Survival Sunday' sees Dowie's side battling it out with Norwich, Southampton and West Brom in a bid to stave off relegation, but it is the Baggies who stay up with a win over Portsmouth. Sadly, the Eagles are held to a 2-2 draw at Charlton and relegation is confirmed. **2006** The play-offs are achieved yet again but Palace lose 3-0 on aggregate against Watford. Iain Dowie departs and Peter Taylor is brought in to replace him. **2007** Taylor leaves the club after a disappointing start to the 2007–08 season and Neil Warnock becomes the latest man to take charge. **2008** Palace keep up the impressive record of reaching the play-offs but bow out in the semi-finals again, this time at the hands of Bristol City. **2009** The start of the 2009–10 season is seriously disrupted as the club is hit with a transfer embargo by the Football League. **2010** The club goes into administration and there is more bad news when Neil Warnock leaves for Queens Park Rangers. It gets worse, too, with Palace sucked into yet another battle against the drop. Under caretaker boss Paul Hart, however, the club hang on by the skin of their teeth and a 2-2 draw against Sheffield Wednesday is enough to keep the Eagles up and send the Owls down. The CPFC 2010 consortium, consisting of Steve Parish, Stephen Browett, Martin Long and Jeremy Hosking, take control of the club and appoint George Burley as first-team manager. **2011** Burley lasts just six months and is sacked after a 3-0 defeat at Millwall. Club legend Dougie Freedman takes over as caretaker manager, before being handed the role on a permanent basis. **2012** Palace lose on penalties to Cardiff City in the Carling Cup semi-final but their good Cup form is not matched in the League. They finish 17th in the Championship. The club make an impressive start to the season under Freedman but there is a major upheaval when he leaves to join Bolton in October. Ian Holloway is named as the new manager. **2013** The club finish the Championship season in fifth to set up a play-off semi-final clash with arch-rivals Brighton & Hove Albion. A 2-0 win at the AMEX Stadium puts Palace 90 minutes away from the top flight and a penalty from veteran striker Kevin Phillips in the showpiece at Wembley fires the club back to the promised land. Palace are a Premier League side for the first time in eight seasons.

Continuing money problems throughout the Nineties saw the club come perilously close to extinction towards the end of the decade under the ownership of financier Mark Goldberg. While Goldberg had owned the club, Ron Noades had retained ownership of Selhurst Park and it was during Goldberg's reign that the Eagles went into administration. In 2000, however, Singaporean financier Jerry Lim bought the club and immediately sold it to 32-year-old mobile phone tycoon Simon Jordan. A lifelong Palace fan who had grown up close to the ground, the flamboyant new owner had something of a rollercoaster time in charge and regularly changed managers during his near-10 years at the club. Perhaps the most high-profile falling-out of Jordan's reign was the one with Iain Dowie. Dowie left Palace and soon after joined Charlton Athletic, prompting Jordan to hit his former manager with a high court writ during the press conference to unveil him as the Addicks' new boss. Jordan won his case against Dowie, claiming he had lied about his reasons for leaving the club, but Dowie appealed and the pair eventually settled their differences out of court. In 2006, Jordan announced that he had bought the freehold for Selhurst Park from Ron Noades, but when Selhurst Park Limited went into administration the CPFC 2010 consortium, led by Steve Parish, purchased the club and the stadium.

Jordan is pictured in 2001, a year after taking over at Palace and (inset), days after buying the club in August 2000, at the unveiling of former manager Alan Smith as the club's new boss.

"The highs and lows of Palace are quite extreme."

Alan Smith

A run to the semi-finals of the League Cup during the 2000–01 season gave Eagles fans something to cheer during what was a difficult campaign. Steve Coppell had resigned as manager just 11 days before the season started and, for a second time, Alan Smith was brought in as his successor. The security which Jordan had brought and the change at the helm buoyed supporters, but, that Cup run aside, results on the field were poor. Palace would face a real fight for their Division One life and it went right down to the final game of the season. However, Dougie Freedman's goal at Stockport gave them a massive victory and saw Huddersfield Town, who had started the day one place above the Eagles, fifth from bottom, go down.

ABOVE Mikael Forssell, who spent two seasons at Palace on loan from Chelsea, makes a point after scoring for Palace in their 2-1 victory over Sunderland in the Worthington Cup quarter-finals in 2000. Jamie Pollock and Craig Harrison (right) enjoy the former's goal against West Bromwich Albion in a 2-2 draw at Selhurst Park on 3rd February 2001, in which Mikael Forssell also scored.

Clinton Morrison had scored the first goal for the Eagles that night and was on target again in the semi-final first leg against Liverpool. Morrison and Andrejs Rubins gave Palace a 2-1 lead from the home game but the Reds won 5-0 at Anfield.

It was great as a young player to go to Palace and gain invaluable experience for my career. It is a great club, with great fans. I look back on my time there with fond memories.

Mikael Forssell

–LEGENDS–

Dougie Freedman

Palace paid £800,000 to take Dougie Freedman from Barnet in 1995 and the Scottish striker became an instant hit with the Selhurst Park faithful by scoring 20 League goals in his first season. A further 11 the following campaign helped Palace win promotion to the Premiership via the play-offs but signified the beginning of the end of his first spell at the club as he was sold to Wolves in October 1997. He returned three years later, this time signing from Nottingham Forest, and would go on to score the goal against Stockport that kept Palace in the second tier. Freedman had a mixture of highs and lows, but became only the seventh player to hit a century of goals for Palace during a 3-2 win over Brighton & Hove Albion on 20th November 2005. He began his coaching career when, in 2007, he took over Palace's reserves, but a loan move to Leeds and a permanent switch to Southend ended his spell in charge. However, he was appointed assistant manager under Paul Hart in March 2010 and stayed on in that capacity when George Burley took over, before replacing his compatriot at the helm in January 2011. Freedman's reign lasted until October 2012, when he left to take over at Bolton Wanderers.

FOOTBALL –STATS–

Dougie Freedman

Name: Dougie Freedman

Born: 21st January 1974 (Glasgow)

Playing career: Barnet, Crystal Palace, Wolverhampton Wanderers, Nottingham Forest, Crystal Palace, Leeds United (loan), Southend United; Scotland

Position: Striker

Palace appearances: 368 (1995–97 and 2000–08)

Palace goals: 108

Scotland appearances: 2

Scotland goals: 1

Freedman fires home the all-important goal for Palace against Stockport on 6th May 2001 to keep them in Division One (left) and celebrates Palace's second in a 3-2 defeat by Portsmouth in Division One on 17th August 2002 with Dele Adebola (above).

"Crystal Palace is a club that will never be too far away from my heart because it gave me the chance to fulfil my professional career at the top level and the opportunity to go into coaching and management. From early in my playing career, it was always in the back of my mind that I would like to manage one day and probably walking out as the manager of Crystal Palace would be the biggest highlight of my time there. I was also very proud to work with the Under-16s and the reserves."

Dougie Freedman

197

Helsinki-born Aki Riihilahti was another foreign import who enjoyed a wonderful relationship with the Selhurst Park faithful. A hard-working and tough-tackling defensive midfielder from Finland who made 178 appearances for the club in all competitions, scoring 14 goals during his six-year stay, Riihilahti won more international caps while playing for Palace than anyone else in the club's history. Riihilahti's intelligence and wit off the field endeared him to Eagles fans every bit as much as his contribution on it, and he became well known for his newspaper columns both in Britain and in his homeland.

Riihilahti in action during a 2-1 defeat to Burnley on 1st December 2001. Clinton Morrison scored the Palace goal that night.

Managers came and went in quick succession at the start of the century with former midfield favourite Steve Kember taking over as caretaker manager from Alan Smith in April 2001 and then again from Steve Bruce in October of the same year. Trevor Francis was installed full-time a month later and, the following April, Kember was back in charge. He lasted until November 2003 and another ex-player, defender Kit Symons, took over for six weeks as caretaker manager before Iain Dowie was brought in just before Christmas that year. Dowie would lead the club to the play-off finals at the Millennium Stadium in Cardiff – Sunderland had been beaten on penalties in the semis after a 4-4 aggregate draw – and Neil Shipperley's goal was enough to once again lift Palace into the Premier League.

Central defender Tony Popovic takes the acclaim of Palace fans at the Millennium Stadium on 29th May 2004. The Aussie made 144 appearances for Palace over five years, scoring eight goals.

–LEGENDS–

Andrew Johnson

Andrew Johnson arrived at Selhurst Park from Birmingham City as a makeweight in the transfer which took Clinton Morrison in the opposite direction in the summer of 2002, although it would soon become the widely held belief that Palace had got the better end of the deal. Johnson hit the ground running and bagged an incredible 10 goals in five games in October and November of the 2002–03 season, including back-to-back hat-tricks in a 5-0 victory over the arch-enemy Brighton & Hove Albion and a 4-3 win at Walsall. His strike-rate dipped somewhat later in that first season and he ended the campaign with 14 goals in all competitions, 11 of them in the League, but in the following campaign he cemented his hero status with the fans. AJ bagged 27 League goals that season as Palace finished sixth to claim a play-off spot and he scored again in the 3-2 first-leg win over Sunderland in the play-offs. Sunderland won the second leg 2-1 to force extra-time but when the two sides still couldn't be separated it went to penalties and the Eagles were triumphant. That shoot-out set up a clash with West Ham United at the Millennium Stadium and Palace won 1-0 to gain promotion. Johnson proved he could cut it in the Premiership the following season with 21 goals in 37 games, although that haul wasn't enough to save Palace from relegation, and he bagged another 15 goals the following season before he was sold to Everton for £8.6 million. In September 2013 Johnson, now at Queens Park Rangers, almost returned to Palace on transfer deadline day but QPR upped their asking price at the 11th hour and the move fell through. The prospective move had set pulses racing among Palace fans, for a couple of hours at least, but Johnson's return wasn't to be.

Johnson's famous burger-eating celebration started after he was rested for a League Cup clash with Charlton at The Valley on 27th October 2004, a game the Eagles won 2-1 thanks to goals from Dougie Freedman and Sándor Torghelle. Johnson got himself a ticket in the away end, sitting alongside the travelling Palace fans, and he was subjected to a barrage of light-hearted banter at the interval when he was spotted queueing up alongside them at one of the fast-food stalls. This picture was taken on 31st January 2004, as he celebrated one of his two goals in a 3-1 victory over Wimbledon. Danny Granville was also on target for Palace.

FOOTBALL
-STATS-

Andrew Johnson

Name: Andrew Johnson

Born: 10th February 1981 (Bedford)

Playing career: Birmingham City, Crystal Palace, Everton, Fulham, Queens Park Rangers; England

Position: Striker

Palace appearances: 160 (2002–06)

Palace goals: 84

England appearances: 8

Shaun Derry congratulates Johnson on a goal against Reading on 6th March 2004 (above), a 2-2 draw in which Dougie Freedman also scored, and Johnson in action in a 0-0 draw with Nottingham Forest at Selhurst Park on 9th November 2002 (left).

In 2005, Palace fans were asked to vote for a Centenary XI. They were given shortlists of 10 players for each position. This is how they voted . . .

Nigel Martyn

Paul Hinshelwood

Jim Cannon

Chris Coleman

Kenny Sansom

John Salako

Geoff Thomas

Andy Gray

Attilio Lombardo

Andrew Johnson

Ian Wright

Wilfried Zaha moved to South London from Ivory Coast aged four and grew up to become one of the most skilful and technically gifted players to pull on a Palace jersey. A tricky winger who joined the club aged 12, he could be infuriating at times, beating several men before putting the cross which followed into the stands, but, boy, did he know how to excite a crowd! It was always apparent that Wilf, as he was known to all at the club, would soon move on to bigger and better things, and so he did four years after caretaker manager Paul Hart, on the advice of Dougie Freedman, handed him his first-team debut as a substitute in a 2-1 defeat by Cardiff City at Selhurst Park on 27th March 2009. In January 2013, Sir Alex Ferguson paid £15 million to take Zaha to Manchester United, loaning him back to Palace for the rest of the season. He played a full part in helping the Eagles to the play-offs and his two goals against arch-rivals Brighton & Hove Albion in the second leg of their semi-final – giving Palace a 2-0 aggregate victory – and his contribution in the final proved the perfect way to say goodbye before he moved to Old Trafford that summer.

BELOW: The *Mirror* records Zaha's first call-up to England's senior squad – as well as interest from then-Real Madrid boss Jose Mourinho – on 13th November 2012, the day before he made his debut as a substitute against Sweden.

RIGHT: Zaha's switch to Manchester United is confirmed in the *Mirror* on 14th January 2013.

Zaha tries to get a cross in during the play-off final victory over Watford on 27th May 2013 but is under pressure from Lloyd Doyley and (left) in action during the same game.

Bright and Shiny Zaha

"One of the best moves I made was to bring in Dougie Freedman and he knew the club inside out. He knew what was coming through and he said, 'We've got this young boy who is really good'. I got Wilf involved in training and we just said, 'Okay, we'll give him a go'. He was a very quiet young man, very humble, but he went on and put on a real good show for such a young chap. I'm delighted we did it. It gave everybody a lift, the supporters, everybody. His ability was not in question and he was destined for great things, we all felt that, and I'm so pleased he has gone on to do just that."

Paul Hart

An Old Maestro . . .

When Palace beat Brighton & Hove Albion in the play-off semi-finals they reached the final for a record fifth time. According to the newspapers, victory and promotion to the Premier League was worth a mind-boggling £120 million, and on a gorgeous day in North London it was the Eagles and their manager Ian Holloway who left the famous stadium smiling. It took Holloway's side 120 minutes to beat the Hornets, but veteran striker Kevin Phillips repaid his gaffer's faith, keeping the coolest of heads to slot home a penalty after Wilfried Zaha had been fouled in extra-time. There were heroes all over the pitch for Palace that day, not least 39-year-old Phillips, skipper Mile Jedinak and defender Damien Delaney.

. . . And a Young One

Attacking midfielder Jonathan Williams basks in the glory of a job well done with manager Ian Holloway following the victory over Watford. A player of great talent, big things are expected of the attacking midfielder, who made his debut aged 17 against Coventry City on 16th August 2011. In 2012, Williams put pen to paper on a five-year contract at Palace, but with the big guns already training their sights on the England-born Wales international, it remains to be seen how long he will stay at Selhurst Park.

> When we got the penalty I was thinking, 'Who's going to take it? [Mile] Jedinak was coming up, and then I saw Kevin was on the pitch and I thought, 'You know what, there's not a better person on this pitch for this moment'.
>
> Danny Gabbidon

> Having the medal around my neck was a great feeling, to be involved with the group of players and [to] go down in the history of Crystal Palace . . . It crowned the year and I think we deserved it.
>
> Jonathan Williams

Premier Palace

Crystal Palace 1-0 Watford,
Wembley Stadium, 27th May 2013.

> *"All I really want is for Crystal Palace to win every game from now until the end of time. That's all. I know that's a tough thing to ask, but that really is what I want."*
>
> Comedian, actor and Palace associate director Eddie Izzard

For Barnaby Winn.

The author would like to thank: Richard Havers for the opportunity and for his guidance, knowledge and suggestions; Simon Flavin, Vito Inglese and the team at Mirrorpix for their invaluable assistance and all at Haynes Publishing; Neil Ashton and Dominic Fifield.

Special thanks again to Kenny Sansom.

Sources: *Crystal Palace: The Complete Record 1905–2011*, Ian King (The Derby Books Publishing Company Ltd); *100 Years of Crystal Palace Football Club*, Nigel Sands (Stadia); *Crystal Palace FC Centenary Book – The History of Crystal Palace in Words and Pictures*, Dominic and Andrew Fifield (Publications UK); *We All Follow The Palace* (Eagle Eye Publications). Newspapers: *Daily Mirror, Sunday Mirror, Sunday People*. Website: www.cpfc.co.uk

Lastly, to Nigel Clarke, Jack Steggles, Kent Gavin, Monte Fresco, Paul Webb, Tony Stenson and all those *Mirror* men and women who have written about and photographed this famous South London club.